*the* Power
*of* Purrs

# *the* Power *of* Purrs

## Reflections on a Life with Cats

GARY SHIEBLER

Foreword by
Kinky Friedman

THE LYONS PRESS
Guilford, CT
*An imprint of The Globe Pequot Press*

The Lyons Press is an imprint of The Globe Pequot Press.

Photos courtesy of the author

Text design by Claire Zoghb

Library of Congress Cataloging-in-Publication Data

Shiebler, Gary.
The power of purrs : reflections on a life with cats / Gary Shiebler.
p. cm.
ISBN 978-1-59921-310-1 (alk. paper)
1. Cats—Anecdotes. 2. Cat owners—Anecdotes.
3. Human-animal relationships—Anecdotes. I. Title.
SF445.5.S54 2008
636.8—dc22
2007050103

Printed in the United States of America

10 9 8 7 6 5 4 3 2 1

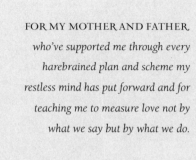

FOR MY MOTHER AND FATHER,
*who've supported me through every*
*harebrained plan and scheme my*
*restless mind has put forward and for*
*teaching me to measure love not by*
*what we say but by what we do.*

# Contents

# Foreword

THIS IS A BOOK ABOUT numerous cats that captured more than mice and lizards; they captured the human heart. If you've never in your life had the good fortune of being possessed by a cat, you may not understand what I'm talking about. You've been spiritually deprived of one of life's greatest experiences, and it's not your fault. It's just another reason why you should read this beautiful book.

Nothing against dogs, of course. I come from a small, ill-tempered family, and my five dogs, the Friedmans, are about as close to having children as I ever plan to get. But while the Friedmans are family to me these days, I'll never forget the three cats that once, many years ago, graced my life. Cuddles, Lady, and Dr. Skat have all crossed the rainbow bridge before me. As sure as night follows day, I know they're waiting for me on the other side. But if I never get to see them again, that would be all right, too. Long ago, I consigned these three loving spirits to my heart.

In reading *The Power of Purrs,* I am struck by the clarity with which the author remembers the cats of his own childhood. That this book is a work of love is beyond question. Shiebler knows well that cats, like childhood itself, never seem to manage to stay with us quite long enough. And (unlike most politicians) they invariably leave with us a warm and wistful legacy of love.

While this is not a good book to read to the Friedmans, it's a great book to read to children or to have children read to you. *The Power of Purrs* paints a compelling portrait of God's most independent-minded creatures, perhaps explaining why Alexander the Great, Napoleon, and Hitler all despised cats. There is something about the perverse, whimsical, freedom-loving nature of the cat that always manages to annoy dictators of virtually every stripe. One more reason, if you need any, to love cats.

If you've never had your life filled with the awkward grace of a feline friend, you, especially, should be required to read this book at gunpoint. Finding a cat—or having a cat find you—can change your world as much as marriage, divorce, love, death, or even winning the lottery can, and sometimes more. Gary Shiebler is not a high-pressure salesman; he just tells the stories simply and well and leaves it up to you to read between the lines. Indubitably, most good writing is done between the lines. That's where cats like to play.

In the meantime, enjoy this book. If you're already fond of cats, you're going to love it. If you're not, you may just learn a thing or two about life, love, and lizards.

—*Kinky Friedman*

# Acknowledgments

To my beloved wife, Linda, and daughter, Hayden. You know the mess I'd be in without you. . . .

To my brother and best friend, Glenn.

To my sister, Susan, and her amazing kids—Michael, Elissa, Matthew, and Christa.

To my manager, Connie Nelson, as good a friend as anyone could ask for.

To all my friends, musicians, songwriters in Nashville and beyond (in no particular order): Jimmy and Pat Johnson; Mike Baker; Martin Parker; Deanie Richardson; Buck and Kathy Jarrell; Tim Atwood; Marcia Ramirez; Craig Campbell; Bobby and Jeannie Bare; Ralph and Joy Emery; Evelyn Shriver; Susan Nadler; Michael Campbell; George and Nancy Jones; Porter and Deb Wagoner; Little Jimmy and Mona Dickens; Jerry Reed; Patty Loveless; Frank Mull; Merle, Theresa, and Ben Haggard; Amy Nelson; Tanya Tucker and the kids—Grayson, Presley, and Layla; Dawn O'Leary; Rich Louv; and all the others I've invariably overlooked.

To all my generous friends and sponsors throughout the years, including Gary and Beverly Yamamoto, Gary and Susan Loomis, Toyo Shimano, Ken Sasaki, Larry Evans, Al Perkinson at Costa Del Mar, Scott Leysath, Julie Schuster at Bass Pro Shops, Mark Wilson, and all the gang from the Fred Hall Shows.

To my literary agent, Sammie Justesen, for believing in second chances.

To my terrific editor, Kaleena Cote, for her vision and tireless efforts to make this project a reality. Thanks for going to bat for me at every turn . . .

A special thanks to Ellen Urban and Eileen Clawson for cleaning up the rough edges so beautifully.

And for every cat that has graced my life.

*purr*

# Introduction

*A home without a cat, and a well-fed, well-petted and*
*properly revered cat, may not be a perfect home,*
*but how can it prove its title?*
—MARK TWAIN

IT'S FIVE O'CLOCK IN THE morning, and I'm in that comfortable in-between place, not quite asleep or awake, that magical drifting and floating place you wish could last forever and where real time passes all too quickly. Soon, the first hints of a new day will begin filtering through the silvery mist in tones of abalone and gold and the walls of our bedroom will slowly reveal themselves in a tender wash of light. The soothing hum of the refrigerator in the kitchen drifts lazily down the hall in the sweet, fading darkness—its efficient motor firmly cooling the half gallon of milk that I'll splash in my strong cup of coffee in a couple of hours. The cheap, digital clock that sits on top of my dresser is a glowing confirmation that I still have a little time to luxuriate in the final strands of a good night's sleep.

Suddenly, the spell is broken. Not by a blaring car horn or a rattling garbage truck hoisting barrels over whining belts and chugging cylinders, but by a surging collage of thumps and gallops growing from the back of the house. I always try to ignore it, but there's no defense against these mischievous stirrings, no covers thick enough to hide under, no bedroom door solid enough to stem this restless, impatient tide. Soon, these furry conquistadors will spill into the hallway, ricochet off the walls, and lay siege to our bedroom. We try our best to turn them away, but there's just no stopping cats that want breakfast.

Through sleepy grunts and sluggish groans, my wife and I reach for anything within an arm's length of our nightstands. In just a few moments, the air in our once-tranquil bedroom will be filled with slippers, socks, pillows, Kleenex boxes, and small inspirational books. It's a noble display, but the cats know that it's just a matter of time before our paltry cache runs dry. They deftly sidestep our halfhearted barrage and dutifully press onward. Soon they'll be on the bed, marching up the entire length of our pajama-covered bodies.

Twitchy tails will swish beneath noses, whiskers will tickle cheeks, and fuzzy heads will poke and prod our chins. If we refuse to surrender, the troops will split up, and valuable glass items and collectables will be pushed off the edges of dresser tops, phones will be pulled off hooks, and miniblinds will be systematically dismantled. If those tactics fail to swing our feet to the floor, they can always "accidentally" brush up against Cielo, our cat-despising fox terrier. There's no better way to propel us toward the kitchen than with a spinning, snarling, predawn brawl at the end of the bed.

Once I'm up, the offensive is immediately called off. The battle has been won, this particular morning's war is over, and I, the defeated mother ship, am carefully escorted to the kitchen by a now-gracious flotilla of whiskered tugboats. When I'm safely in port, the cats strategically reposition themselves on counters and breakfast bars and quietly wait for the familiar sound of cabinet doors opening and silverware drawers sliding out. The recognizable metallic puff of the can opener and my slow, wristy grind around a fresh serving of ocean whitefish signal the end of another successful ground campaign.

I've often wondered why I'm so tolerant of these early-morning blitzkriegs. Perhaps it's because I'd rather be awakened by a sea of cat paws and a chorus of meows than by the jarring pulses of a plastic digital alarm clock. What's more, my day begins with an act of giving, which is always a good way to start a day.

The following stories are but a slender testimony to these remarkable and often misunderstood feline companions. And when I think of the array of richness, vitality, comfort, and color they've brought to my life, I have to go way back to the beginning. To a cat named Sweet Kitty.

*purr*

*the* Power
*of* Purrs

# CHAPTER 1

# Sweet Kitty

THERE WERE THREE UNWRITTEN laws at 17 Orchard Road.

First, when it came to jazz clarinetists, you couldn't mention Benny Goodman and Artie Shaw in the same sentence.

"Nobody can touch Benny," my dad would regularly proclaim. "Nobody."

Second, all pizza came from Donato's.

"Go pick up the pie with your father," my mom would always say. "You know how much Dominick and Nancy love to see you."

The remaining mandate was this: At no time would there be fewer than two cats and two dogs in our household.

My mother and father adored animals. In their eyes, a home without pets was just a house. Their benevolent decree seemed divinely aided, for every time we lost a dog or cat, another would always magically appear on our doorstep. And though I've often heard the phrases "dog person" and "cat person," my mother and father were neither. They reaped the harvests of both, celebrated their differences, accepted the chaos their relationships hosted, and loved them all with equal abandon.

"Dogs are like coffee, cats are like tea," my mother would often say. "There will be many times in your life, no doubt, when your dogs will be

**Sweet Kitty**

your best friend." Then she'd add, "But never underestimate the power of purrs."

Growing up in that loving home, outside of my dogs and cats, there were few things I treasured more in the world than my blue Schwinn bicycle. Whether I was skimming through glassy puddles after a spring rain, soaring above sidewalk panels turned into launching ramps by swollen tree roots, or just riding up and down the driveway, my Schwinn was my silver-spoked magic carpet—my suburban steed. I tasted many of my first true moments of freedom, exhilaration, and danger riding atop that sensible and sturdy frame.

One of my favorite places to ride was right next door to my house. Bianchi's Wholesale Greenhouses was a mysterious, spooky place—a world filled with long shadows and peculiar sounds. Rows and rows of strange flowers bloomed beneath ghostly concourses of whitewashed windows, and chestnut-skinned men made fertilizer and sang songs under the hot August sun in languages I couldn't understand. It was a maze of secret paths and alleys where a boy could ride his bicycle for as long as he wished; a place ripe with magic and filled with cats, secret cats that only came out at night so as never to be seen or caught. I used to catch glimpses of them from my bedroom window, darting from behind tractors or scaling bales of peat in the light of the moon. I always hoped that one might be brave or curious enough to jump over the fence into our yard.

One day, my wish came true.

"She must have come from Bianchi's," my mom said. "I found her out by the garage while I was hanging the laundry. It looked like her tail had been run over by a car or something. Took her up to the vet right away. We didn't have any choice *but* to keep her."

It seemed that Mom said that about every stray that showed up in our yard. There was no such thing as the pound. There was also no such thing as a bad name.

When it comes to naming cats, there's a bottomless well of exotic and unconventional names to choose from. In naming a dog, you have to be more practical. The simpler, more monosyllabic the name, the better and the more likely the dog is to understand commands and obey. Since getting the attention of a cat requires a whole different set of inflections and attitude, these rules do not apply; hence "Edgar Allan Paws" is a totally acceptable name for a cat. It wouldn't, however, fly too well if you were trying to call your black lab home for dinner.

"She was sweet, and she was a kitty," my father said, defending his choice of names. This came from the same man who, when a gorgeous black Persian wandered into our yard one November morning when I was twelve, lobbied for the name "New Black Kitty." I'm glad my mother had the final say in naming their children.

Whether it was tending to the three litters of kittens she'd eventually bear or curling up next to the freshly clawed nose of our dog, Rusty (courtesy of an unprovoked encounter with her evil feline stepsister, Cokie), Sweet Kitty was the rock and ever-nurturing mother cat of my childhood. Plump yet solid, she was somewhere between a striped and a spotted tabby. The loss of her tail only accentuated her rotund and matronly appearance. But she was built well, not easily ruffled, definitely more Mammy than Scarlett O'Hara, and her steady and calm demeanor seemed to soften the edges of our often-frantic household.

Her coat was the typical tabby blend of blacks, browns, and grays with ocelot-like spots running down her back and along her sides. These oblong markings conjoined at the top of her rump with a series of tiger stripes that spilled wildly down her ample flanks and thighs to sandy paws. Her soft, gentle face was much too small for the great bouquet of whiskers that sprang from her ivory muzzle, and her large, sharp ears completely dominated the top of her narrow head. Painted between those ears just above her brow was a series of lines and stripes that formed the perfect letter "M," a fitting insignia for this grand matriarch.

We learned quickly that her defection from the greenhouse was not a clean break, due in part to a big, black tom that usually held court at the base of the huge brick smokestack that helped heat the greenhouses in winter. For three successive springs, she'd disappear for a few days, only to grace us two months later with a fresh batch of newborns, always delivered under my parents' bed.

Her delivery regime was always the same: each time she'd stroll belly-heavy into my parents' bedroom—usually just before they were getting ready to go out to dinner—let out a throaty meow, arch her back, disappear under the bed, and emerge on the other side with a damp new arrival in her gentle mouth. All of her broods were identical—one gray, one black, and one tiger. Often in heels and stockings, my mother would hastily prepare the bottom drawer of my father's dresser by lining it with towels and receiving blankets from when I was a baby, and for the next six weeks, the former repository for my dad's pajamas would become a mewing nest of furry faces.

Although my mom complained each time Sweet Kitty was pregnant, I could always detect a certain excitement and comfort in her eyes. And as much as I support the need for spay and neuter programs, I can't help but think that's something's lost when we don't allow our children to experience at least one litter of kittens in their lifetimes. I think my mom felt the same way. It's a precious process to see a mother nurse her newborns—to watch their eyes slowly open and their personalities emerge. Each morning when I woke up, I couldn't wait to see the kittens, to hold my favorite one and hear all of their tiny mews.

Even the process of finding them homes was a joy, as my mother hand-stenciled tiny birth certificates for each one and made collars out of ribbon bearing colorful nametags. As a result, Sweet Kitty's kittens always got adopted, and we received permanent imprints on our hearts as to the power of love, responsibility, and the importance of having cats in our lives at all times.

As soon as their eyes were fully open and legs not too wobbly, it was time to go to "school." The middle of our kitchen floor was where Sweet Kitty taught her lessons, and every morning after breakfast she'd gather up her young pupils, march them to the front of the stove, and lecture them on the finer points of stalking and hunting. On the days she decided to teach a lab, it was not unusual for her to bring in a live subject from the backyard, flapping and flailing about on the linoleum floor. With all three litters, she was strict and extremely committed to her curriculum. One might imagine her teaching schedule looking something like this:

Mondays and Wednesdays, 8–10 a.m.: "Fundamentals of Mousing"
Tuesdays, 1–3 p.m.: "Bird Feeders: A Cat's Best Friend"
Thursdays, 9–11 a.m.: "Moles, Voles, and Gophers—The Other
    Brown Meat"
Fridays, 8–10 a.m.: "Avoiding Cokie: The Meanest Cat in the World"

When classes were over, my mother would play janitor to Sweet Kitty's graphic presentations and dutifully clean up the smorgasbord of feathers, spleens, and fur scattered beneath cabinets and under barstools. One morning she made the mistake of carrying an overflowing laundry basket through the kitchen in her bare feet without watching where she was going. Suddenly, she felt something warm and gushy rise up between her toes. Immediately tossing the basket aside, she looked down and much to her horror saw the pancaked remains of a rabbit head, probably from one of Sweet Kitty's evening classes.

Although she was gracious and kind to us all, there was never any doubt that Sweet Kitty was my mother's cat. They seemed to share a deep and common bond—a maternal understanding that there was no greater purpose in life than staying close to home and raising a family. And when my parents' marriage was on the brink of falling apart, almost terminally strained by money woes and seventy-two-hour workweeks, it was Sweet Kitty that helped my mother through the longest nights of despair. I'd often see them sitting together in the rocker by the fireplace after a particularly harsh fight, my mom lost in a tearful, faraway gaze. It was a sad yet strangely reassuring sight, for it left a permanent impression as to how important our cats can be, particularly when we've been hurt or betrayed by our own kind. And while I'm not sure what role Sweet Kitty played in saving my parents' marriage (they recently celebrated their fifty-fifth wedding anniversary), I'm confident of one thing: she was one of the few things my mom could depend on in a time when most things were falling apart.

When Sweet Kitty was twelve, during a routine checkup, Dr. Francis Barry, our devoted veterinarian, discovered a cancerous growth on her left front leg. Despite her age and the fact that my folks had little money, there was never any question about what needed to be done. She was family, an immeasurable part of our daily existence, and my parents vowed to do everything they could to save her.

The operation was a success, but it cost her the use of that leg. Over time, she learned to compensate for the loss. I'll never forget how bravely and determinedly she'd struggle up into visitors' laps or hobble down stairwells, as if to demonstrate her gratitude for getting a second chance.

And although it was uncomfortable and awkward, particularly in the beginning, the cast that she had to wear on her leg for the first few months proved to be the perfect solution to Cokie's sneak attacks. If bothered, Sweet Kitty would simply turn around and club her over the head. Needless to say, Cokie never bothered Sweet Kitty again.

It's easy to appreciate the value of a dog that greets a young boy on a front lawn after school: leaping, bounding, tail wagging, tongue dangling, and eyes beaming. It's not as easy to mark the importance of a sleeping cat curled up on a cobbler's bench next to where you drop your book bag every day. Sweet Kitty was my trusted anchor. Her simple and steady presence helped me believe, even in the most uncertain times, that everything was going to be all right. And while most of my memories of her have faded into a blurry tapestry of snapshots and lore, reminiscences of a life that surrounded her remain vivid.

I want to go back to that small house next to the old flower-filled greenhouses.

I want to stand on frosty steps in my pajamas and call my cat's name just like my father used to do.

"Sweeeeeeet Kitty . . . Sweeeeeeet Kitty. . . ."

I want to see her bound up out of the darkness and disappear between my slippered feet and into the house. I want to pick her up, feel her weight in my arms, and explore her coat with my fingers. I want to stop for a moment, look into her eyes, catalog her meow, and memorize her purr. I want to tell her about a boy's life, those barreling, leaping, tumbling days that tatter the knees of blue jeans and scrape elbows. A boy's life, where everything moves so fast and playing King of the Hill and wrestling with dogs reign supreme. A life of taking things for granted, of racing in and out of doors, of riding bicycles, and running past things in a blur.

Yes, a boy's life.

*purr*

# CHAPTER 2

# Timothy

TO GET TO KNOW A CAT, you need two things: space and time. At the Helen Woodward Animal Center, where I taught elementary and middle school students about pet responsibility and care, we usually didn't have enough of either. And while, after a few days, it's fairly easy to get a read on the personality of a newly surrendered dog, cats are much more stingy and protective about revealing anything about themselves.

In fact, it might take a few weeks before they want to have anything to do with people. They often retreat into the farthest corners of their cages and enter a shutdown mode—a strange kind of semiconscious trance. My gentle scratches and soft words had little effect on breaking through their protective shields, and I began to realize that most new cats just wanted to be left alone.

"Take care of their basic needs every day, and eventually they'll warm up to you," a seasoned volunteer told me one morning.

And so I cleaned cages, changed litter boxes, and filled food bowls, consciously making an effort to avoid any physical contact for fear of disturbing them. Sometimes, I'd accidentally brush my arm against a curled-up back, and there'd be a quick turn of a head and an icy glare. I certainly understood their displeasure. The silver-barred quarantine

Timothy

cages that were their temporary homes for the first week were stark and small, and the steady flow of peering faces and well-intentioned, high-pitched greetings that passed by each day must have seemed like a bad dream to most. In time, all but a few would emerge from their spells and warm up to the wiggling fingers searching for neck scratches through the bars.

Timothy would be one of the exceptions. My heart sank the first day I read his adoption card: *Timothy is a seven-year-old male tabby who has had a very difficult life. He needs a loving, quiet home, preferably with no children. He is very shy but will undoubtedly warm up to someone willing to give him the love and care he deserves.*

"They found him locked in a freezer on a back porch," a volunteer told me as I was reading the card in front of his cage. "A couple of teen-age boys had been abusing him for a month."

A shorthaired tabby with an unusual but handsome blend of muted browns, tans, and cinnamons, Timothy never once let me see his face. He stayed curled up in the farthest corner and despite my attempts to draw him out, he most likely didn't feel safe or secure enough to even acknowledge me.

A deep and powerful anger rushed through my veins. Of course, I wanted to find the two criminals, string them up from the nearest canyon oak, skin them alive, and see how *they* felt about living in a Frigidaire for a few days. But that impulse passed quickly, and I thought of the challenge at hand—a cat that seemed permanently damaged and forever withdrawn from a very cruel world.

"I'm not sure he's going to make it," the volunteer added. "He hasn't moved for almost a week."

And so I decided to make Timothy my project. I was driven by two things—first, a belief that most living creatures can be healed by love, regardless of the amount of abuse or neglect they've endured, and second, an aching memory from my childhood. . . .

When I was growing up, there was a rather effeminate boy who lived across the street from our house. For years my friends and I made fun of him and belittled his every move. One day we made up this plan to ask him to play football with us. We knocked on his front door, talked to him in sincere tones, and convinced him to come along and join us. Just as he was getting ready to head outside, we all ran away across his front lawn laughing and screaming. Afterwards, I remember standing in the middle of the street, watching tears run down his face through the glass storm door and feeling a little bit sick inside. It wasn't enough to make me stop teasing him that day, but it showed me, for the first time, that I had the power to really hurt people. And little did I know that a few years later, as a gawky, clarinet-playing teenager in the marching band, I'd regularly be ridiculed and laughed at by football players and cheerleaders, so much bigger and more popular than I was.

As I stood in front of Timothy's cage that morning, for some reason, I thought of that boy across the street. Maybe it was because Timothy reminded me of the cat he used to play with on his front porch after school each day. Maybe it was triggered by what those two boys had done or memories of those horrible days in the marching band. Whatever the reason, that Friday morning, I made a commitment to find the perfect home for Timothy.

But when I returned to work the following Monday, Timothy's cage was empty. I slowly walked back to the cattery, fully expecting the worst.

"I guess Timothy didn't make it," I said quietly to one of the animal technicians.

"Oh, no, he's fine," she said, looking over at me while rinsing out a silver water bowl. "He was adopted Sunday morning."

I couldn't believe it! I flew out the door and ran up to the front desk. One of the adoption counselors was on duty. He was busy talking on the phone.

"If you're looking for kittens, now's the time to come by. We've got about twenty. Yep, *twenty*, in all kinds, all colors, both male and female. Yep, it's definitely springtime . . . " he said into the receiver. "Thank you for calling."

"Timothy got adopted?" I asked excitedly, almost interrupting.

"Yep, went home yesterday."

"Who?" I asked curiously.

"A middle-aged woman. Said she knew just how Timothy felt."

I walked back to my office with a little spring in my step. Soon, a group of fourth and fifth graders would show up for a tour of the shelter. I'd take them back to see the kittens and the puppies and talk about the importance of being a responsible pet owner. I'd probably swing by the rescue stables outside to show off the two llamas we'd just adopted for the education department. I'd let them pet the goat and the miniature donkey for a while. I'd also make sure to spend a few minutes talking about spaying and neutering and how important it is to love and care for our pets. And most likely I'd take a little detour and show them an empty silver cage by a water fountain and perhaps tell them a story about a boy I used to know and a cat that just went home.

*purr*

# CHAPTER 3

# Cokie

PETE WENNER'S FATHER WAS a policeman. George Van Schaick's father was a mechanic. Kenny Drumm's father was a truck driver.

My dad was a disk jockey.

For the first eighteen years of my life, my father worked at WALK, a small AM/FM radio station overlooking the Great South Bay on eastern Long Island. His show, *Memories in Melody*, broadcast six days a week from ten to noon, featured the big-band sounds of the 1930s and 1940s and was the centerpiece of the station's daily programming. On Saturday mornings I'd often bring my friends down to the station to sit in on his show. We'd quietly file into the studio, our eyes glued to the red and white ON AIR sign above the door. If that light started to blink, we'd freeze, barely breathing, truly believing that an errant squeak of a chair or muffled giggle would ruin the entire show. As my father talked smoothly and personally to faces we could only imagine, we'd shift our eyes to his left hand, the tips of his fingers gently holding back the grooves of a freshly cued Count Basie record, the felt turntable spinning quietly beneath.

" . . . So if anyone has seen this cute little black-and-white kitty, please call us here at the station at Grover 5-5200. She answers to the name of 'Missy,' and she's wearing a pink collar with a silver tag. That's

Grover 5-5200. Well, that takes care of the lost dogs and cats for today. And speaking of cats, this is one of the coolest cats of them all. Take it away, Count. . . ."

The first bars of "One O'clock Jump" would leap from the speakers mounted high in the corners of the main studio, the red light would stop blinking, indicating that we were free to breathe and laugh and move our restless bones until it was time for my father to once again cast his magic spell over people sipping coffee at dining-room tables or daydreaming behind big steering wheels at traffic lights.

I'm not sure what it is about the radio business that attracts, shall we say, such an interesting cross-section of people. Whatever it is, one thing is for certain: my childhood was filled with some of the most colorful, off-the-wall characters you could imagine. And of all the outrageous people that worked at the station, there was one who towered over the rest.

"He's the meanest, most obnoxious man on the face of the earth," Grace Breen, the station's humorless receptionist, would regularly proclaim.

With an office just inside the front door, Phil Roll was the radio station's flamboyant traffic and program manager and ersatz maître d'. He was unavoidably my first stop whenever I came to visit my father, his unrestrained and theatrical greeting always drawing me inside his open office door.

"Gary, my dear boy!" he'd bellow from behind his desk, piled chest high with papers. "How the hell are you?"

Every moment of Phil's life was a miniature screen test, every conversation worthy of an Oscar nomination. He'd often show up for work in lime green slacks and cream-colored Angora turtlenecks. Or cranberry blazers with pink Oxford shirts and penny loafers without socks. And he was one of the few people that I've ever known who didn't look totally preposterous wearing an ascot.

Ridiculously thin and perpetually gaunt, he didn't so much walk as teeter along on his toes. He was rarely without a cigarette or drink in hand, and when he inhaled, I imagined smoke penetrating every corner of his wiry frame. Trips to the coffee machine were always an adventure, his pencil-thin legs and reedy arms threatening to betray him at any moment. He'd often leave a trail of creamy splotches on the linoleum floor behind him, completely unconcerned about the slippery mess, confident that some commoner or peasant would take care of it at a later time. Since I had been hired as the janitor for the radio station, it was usually me.

But I didn't mind. I delighted in his royal behavior and his constant quest to outrage and offend. I loved the mischievous gleam in his wide eyes, his tomahawk nose that was much too big for his drawn face, the dashing sideburns that swept across his wide ears and his curly salt-and-pepper hair that spilled down the back of his neck, much too long for a man his age. I marveled at his fingernails, so impeccably clean and clipped, and his lean and elegant hands that seemed to work in tandem with every word that flowed from his mouth. On his right hand he wore a ring, a heavy, silver ring with a burgundy-colored stone inlay that hypnotized me every time he shook my hand or reached for the phone. I would not be the only member of my family that would fall under the spell of that ring. . . .

Although he was considered a good friend and a regular guest for cocktails and dinner in our home, Phil was not the easiest person to be around. He could be stubborn, arrogant, gossipy, and downright mean. As a result my mother and he didn't always get along. Sometimes they would go for weeks without talking to each other.

"He's nothing but a royal pain in the ass," Mom would declare on more than one occasion. "Frankly, I don't care if he ever steps foot in this house again." However, the next day they'd be in the kitchen, sampling wines and dicing shallots for that evening's *blanquette de veau*.

Another point of contention was animals. Mom loved them. Phil hated them. Especially cats.

"Dorothy, darling," he'd pronounce before coming over for cocktails. "Please make sure that all of your animals are in their proper quarters before I arrive." Dutifully, Mom would gather them all together and put them on the screened porch—all except one, the meanest, most obnoxious cat on the face of the earth.

The Marlene Dietrich of felines—stealthy, wicked, and mysterious—Cokie (whose name was inspired by the word "coke"—not the soda, but the jet black residue left over from the mining of coal) was our very own Halloween poster cat, the one seen on every cardboard decoration and greeting card. Back arched, eyes glowing yellow above sharp ivory whiskers and fangs, she'd be the perfect contender for a witch's best friend. For seventeen years this black and sinewy phantom terrorized our home, carving her signature on the noses of curious dogs and randomly scaring the daylights out of unsuspecting dinner guests. In an East Coast suburban neighborhood bereft of rattlesnakes, black widow spiders, or mountain lions, she was a respected source of fear and danger, and her unpredictable presence brought an element of adventure and intrigue into our secure, Dutch colonial home. Some of us still have scars to prove it.

My mother often said that Cokie didn't have a tender bone in her body and that her moments of sweetness and kindness were usually calculated setups for a healthy scratch or swipe.

"Picking her up is like handling a woolly time bomb," my mother said. "She has always been a royal pain in the ass in that regard."

Born in a trailer park in Lake Ronkonkoma, New York, Cokie was one of eight kittens whose mother was killed by a car when they were just six weeks old.

As a kitten Cokie refused to be litter trained and chose to take care of her business in the darkest spot of the farthest corner of the basement. After a while, my mom and dad stopped fighting with her and just put newspapers down.

Of course, it became *my* job to clean up those newspapers in that spooky basement beneath the ghostly quilt of cobwebs and dancing daddy longlegs spiders. And while I had overcome most of my fears about going down there, Cokie would always be lurking in the shadows, waiting to attack my leg just to keep things interesting.

She's managed to become somewhat of a legend in our family. The two black-and-white photographs we have left of her only augment her mystique. In one she is crouched down on a tiled kitchen counter, head tilted, her cavernous mouth wide open, teeth gleaming, eyes rolled back, preparing to tear at the leg of what appears to be the feeble remains of a Thanksgiving or Christmas day turkey. The picture has the hurried feel of having been taken by someone who has stumbled upon a fresh kill on the African Plains, Cokie being the proud lioness that has just taken down her victim. With salt and pepper shakers and dirty carving knives scattered in the foreground, she is clearly thinking, *Snap all the pictures you want, pal. Just don't get too close.*

The second photograph is fuzzy, out of focus, and overexposed—obviously also taken in a hurry. She is crookedly captured in the upper-right-hand corner of the frame, ears cut off, body cropped in half. She appears to be sitting on top of a radiator cover. Her front paws are tucked neatly under her chest, and her head is swiveled awkwardly toward the camera. The hair is up on her back, and her eyes—fiercely hugging the tops of her brows—are shooting flaming arrows of discontent at whoever the poor, unsuspecting photographer is. One can easily imagine a large, claw-filled paw filling the frame of the following exposure.

I'd like to be able to say that, despite all these menacing traits, there were moments when she softened and let down her guard. There weren't—with one peculiar exception . . . she slept with me every night.

As a boy I was very afraid of the dark. I didn't like to sleep alone, and each night, before I turned out the light, I'd call Cokie's name three times. Within moments her shadowy figure would appear in the door-way, and in one fantastic leap she'd disappear under the covers by my knees. And despite her horrible reputation, in all the years that she slept by my side, never once did she bite or scratch me. With my perfect dog, Rusty, at the end of my bed and Cokie curled up in the crook of my

Cokie

plaid-pajama-covered leg, I was as safe and content as any boy could ever be.

In the morning, she'd always be gone; her few hours of tenderness would become just a memory or maybe even a dream. Life with Cokie would quickly return to normal . . . a life where nothing was safe, not arms, legs, feet, turkey carcasses, sleeping dogs, photographers—or large silver rings dangling from fingers on the sides of rocking chairs.

Now, aside from being a regular dinner and after-work-cocktail guest, Phil was as much a fixture in our home on Christmas day as were the roast turkey, creamed onions, and Avon soaps on a rope. I think my mom felt sorry for him, especially during the holidays, as he had no family nearby.

For almost twenty years, martini in hand, he'd hold court from his throne, a thick-runged rocking chair that sat directly off the dining room, dueling with holiday guests over the merits of a local restaurant or a recent opening at the Met. He was our very own correspondent from the *National Enquirer,* a modern-day Hedda Hopper in slacks, and it was guaranteed that at some point in the evening my poor Aunt Ruth would come staggering into the kitchen after hearing one too many of Phil's gossip-barbed revelations about one of her favorite Hollywood actors.

"I refuse to believe those stories about Randolph Scott," she'd mutter to my father, who was usually busy making another double vodka martini for our resident Rex Reed. "Please say it isn't so, Ellsworth. Say it isn't so!"

"Don't believe a word of it," Dad would bark back. "The man's a royal pain in the ass."

Anyone who dared sit in the living room with Phil on Christmas night was bound to be offended at least once during the course of the evening, and his rank comments drove many a houseguest to a premature donning of an overcoat and an early departure. By ten o'clock everyone had usually left, and my mother and Phil would sit together in the holiday afterglow, sip wine, and reminisce about the day. Little did Phil know that directly behind his rocking chair, brilliantly camouflaged in the dim light beneath the dining-room table, was a black phantom— waiting for the perfect moment.

Cokie was well aware of the fact that Phil had no clue as to her whereabouts and that the three martinis he had downed had long since erased any memories of her previous Christmas-night attacks. Confident and sure, she'd silently weave her way through the spindled legs of the maple dining-room chairs, positioning herself for a clear shot to the rocker. The deeply braided colonial rug and dark oak baseboards provided a flawless backdrop for her silent siege. Her mission was simple: get the ring, that big silver ring that tempted and tortured her year after year.

Her assault would be swift and precise. Oh, she might take a swipe at the cuff of Phil's lime green pants upon her retreat, but the plan was clear: get in and get out as quickly as possible. She'd use the spacious pulses of the blinking Christmas-tree lights as her stopwatch. Go for the prize on green, bite on red, and be safely back in the basement on blue.

As in every year, Phil never knew what hit him. He'd make the fatal mistake of setting down his glass of wine, lighting a cigarette, and letting his bejeweled hand casually dangle from the side of the rocker for a moment as he exhaled his first puff. That was all the time Cokie needed. She was on the ring and gone before Phil landed back in his seat.

"That little bitch!" Phil would wail. My mother would quickly come to his aid and curse Cokie in absentia for getting ashes on the rug, but inside she'd be secretly filled with glee.

"I consider it payback for all those things he says about Cary Grant," she would say later on, after Phil had gone home. "She's my little furry avenger."

One might wonder why we tolerated such a difficult man for so many years.

"For all his faults," my mom would say, "he was always very generous in teaching me about 'worldly' things—French cuisine, fine wines, antiques, high fashion, collectibles, and art. And he always brought me something special from Madison Avenue whenever he went into the city," she'd add. "He never forgot to do that."

As Phil got older, he began to fall apart physically. Since he didn't drive, my mother, always generous to a fault, would volunteer to take him to the doctor. After a series of small strokes, the orders were firm: no more drinking, smoking, fatty foods, or sex.

"Dorothy, darling," he protested. "What the hell *else* is there to live for?"

One night, after a visit to the clinic, he came over for dinner. He was his usual belligerent self and spent most of the evening proclaiming that Jerome Hines was indeed the "definitive Don Giovanni."

"God help anyone who even *attempts* to play that part again," was his decree. Oh, how he adored the opera and the ballet.

Later that night, as my mother was walking him to the car, he stopped in the middle of the lawn. He confessed that he hadn't been feeling well lately.

"Dorothy, dear," he whispered, "please hold me; I'm so afraid."

And under the grand old sugar maple in our front yard, the meanest man in the world wept in my mother's arms like a little boy. And just upstairs, in a bedroom that flirted with the top of that tree, a boy would slowly drift off to sleep, with the meanest cat in the world tucked under the covers, right by his side.

*purr*

# CHAPTER 4

# Lady Grey

ON THE FIRST DAY OF summer camp at the center, it was a requirement for my older fifth- and sixth-grade students to "adopt" a shelter pet for the week. It was a critical part of my curriculum, as I wanted each boy and girl to leave the shelter with a permanent stamp on their hearts as to what happens when you leave a dog or cat behind. True, the Helen Woodward Animal Center is one of the finest facilities in the country, and a homeless pet would be hard pressed to find a more loving or responsible place to be. Still, it's a prison of sorts, complete with bars, cells, and the daily stresses that come from having your freedom taken away.

It's for this reason that I insisted on regular contact between the animals and the students. I knew that for many, the hour or so each boy and girl spent with them every day not only lifted the spirits of the animals, but it also made them more adoptable and kept hopes alive that a new home was not far away.

When it came to deciding whether to choose a dog or cat for the week, the results were the same throughout the summer. For every ten students that chose a dog, there were two who wanted to be with the cats. And although there were always a few who wavered in between, there was little or no waffling with the "cat kids." Steadfast and passionate, they were myopic in their resolve and could barely restrain themselves when it came to their desire to hold and comfort their furry choices. They'd literally beg to have the cat cages opened on the first day. I'd try to explain to them how stressful the surroundings were, particularly for the newcomers, and that it would take at least a few days of seeing their faces and hearing their voices through the bars before I'd feel comfortable with letting them out. Most reluctantly agreed to be patient and wait.

And then there was Kate.

Precocious, bright, and with a head of chin-length brown hair that seemed to forever bounce and bob, Kate came from an extremely wealthy family in Rancho Santa Fe. I got a taste of her exotic and chaotic life when, on the first day, I received detailed instructions from Kate's limousine driver as to what her transportation arrangements were for the week.

"Now on Monday she'll be picked up by the nanny. Tuesday and Wednesday her stepmother will come by. She drives a silver Lexus. Please make sure Kate's ready a little early on those days as she needs to get back to work. Thursday it will either be me or her birth mother, who's flying into town for a few days. We still haven't figured out Friday yet. It will probably be her father, but that depends on if he's back from Brazil in time. If not, we'll send the gardener over."

Two days later Kate wrote a poem about what it must be like living at the shelter. I couldn't help but think that she knew exactly how the animals felt:

*It's sad and lonely*
*It makes my heart start pounding*
*like I'm going to be alone forever . . .*

Always volunteering to help pass out worksheets or pencils, she could barely sit still for more than five minutes, and her fetching smile and eager blue-green eyes made it hard to get angry with her during the times she refused to listen or settle down. She was brave, fearless, and extremely knowledgeable when it came to animals, and she always had a front-row seat every Friday when we fed the live mouse to the classroom snake. While other students and volunteers would hide their eyes or run out of the room, Kate would get as close to the glass as possible as the rosy boa slowly swallowed its prey. She'd often turn around and look up at me with a smile and a look that seemed to say, *Isn't this just amazing?*

She was always correcting me during class, and I had to be particularly careful when it came to lessons about cats.

"Now the origin of the Abyssinian has been traced back to ancient Egypt," I'd lecture, only to be quickly corrected by Kate.

"Not true, Mr. Shiebler," she'd blurt out with conviction. "Most scholars believe they were first born and bred in Ethiopia."

She also knew her stuff when it came to the big cats.

"Now here's a picture of the African lion. Known as 'King of the Beasts,' it's the largest cat in the world. . . ."

"Excuse me, Mr. Shiebler," Kate would inform me while scribbling along the top of her notebook. "Lions aren't the biggest cats in the world—tigers are. They can grow up to six hundred pounds. The biggest lions only reach about five hundred pounds."

So I was off by a hundred pounds.

When it came to actually choosing their pets for the week, the process was fairly simple. I took them out to the kennels and the cattery on the first day, led them around single file past each animal, and had them stop and read the cage or kennel identification and history cards. I encouraged them during the first walk through to be quiet and mostly observe and to be on the lookout for the older dogs and cats, as they were the ones, in my eyes, that deserved the most love and attention. I'd then set each boy and girl free to meet and spend time with their choices.

Needless to say, I wasn't surprised when Kate headed straight for the cage that housed one of the more challenging feline personalities at the center—a beautiful, pewter-coated, strong-willed goddess named Lady Grey.

Lady Grey

Lady Grey had been at the center for over six months. After living with a family for almost seven years, she had been surrendered because her owners were moving.

"To a planet where they don't allow cats," Pat, the adoptions manager, would often comment whenever someone brought in a pet because they couldn't be bothered to take care of it anymore.

Lady Grey's reputation for being a tough customer was well deserved, as most of the volunteers would only clean her cage while wearing heavy gloves and long-sleeved shirts. But this didn't faze Kate. She picked Lady Grey right away as her pet for the week and begged me to open her cage and let her hold her right then and there.

"I'd be in a bad mood, too, if somebody gave up on me after seven years," she said. And so she sat with Lady Grey every day, talked to her through the wire mesh of the caged front door, and tried to coax her out of her corner on the shelf by the window. I'm not sure if Lady Grey even turned around to look at her the entire week. But Kate never gave up.

When the week was over, I'd take pictures of each student with their adopted dog or cat. For many it was the highlight of the week (as were the Popsicle-stick picture frames they crafted and painted for their snapshots). The amazing amount of love and care they put into those simple frames was another heartwarming validation of the power that dogs and cats can have in helping us connect with the more generous and compassionate parts of ourselves.

The photo sessions, however, weren't without their problems. There were some dogs and cats that I couldn't trust outside their kennels or cages. It was just too risky. Lady Grey was one of them.

"I don't want a picture with a kitten! I want a picture with Lady Grey!" Kate wailed when I told her about my decision. And so, when I left Kate and the other students in the cattery in order to take pictures of a few of the other kids with their dogs, my instructions were clear: *under no circumstances should anyone open any cages until I get back.*

I wasn't gone five minutes when a couple of breathless students ran up to me.

"Mr. Shiebler, Mr. Shiebler! You better come quick! Something's happened to Kate!" I dropped my camera and sprinted back to the cattery. There, standing in front of Lady Grey's cage, was Kate. There was blood dripping down her right arm, and she was crying hysterically.

I gathered her up in my arms and carried her to my office. There were three long gashes on the inside of her right arm, extending from her elbow joint to her wrist. Kate continued to sob.

"Oh, Mr. Shiebler, please . . . Mr. Shiebler, please. . . ."

"It's all right, Kate, it's OK," I said, trying to calm her down. There was no need to ask what had happened. I already knew. Still, Kate was inconsolable. At first, I thought it was because of the pain from her scratches. But it wasn't.

"Oh, please, Mr. Shiebler, is anything going to happen to her? She won't be put to sleep, will she? Oh, please, it wasn't her fault. She jumped right back into her cage. She just didn't want to be picked up, that's all. Oh, please, Mr. Shiebler, promise me that nothing bad is going to happen to her. . . ." I put a warm washcloth on the inside of her arm and marveled at what mattered most to this little girl.

"Don't worry, Kate," I said. "Nothing bad is going to happen to her." I opened a bottle of hydrogen peroxide and poured some onto a paper towel.

"Now this may sting a little," I warned. She looked up at me through tears.

"It wasn't her fault," she whispered.

We waited at a picnic table near the parking lot together that day for almost an hour. As usual, she would be the last one to be picked up. I had my speech ready for her parents, covering all the details of the incident, how all the cats have been vaccinated, and how I'd cleaned the wounds thoroughly and that there was little risk of infection with sensible and proper care.

"I'll wear long-sleeved shirts until it gets better," Kate assured me, reaching inside her backpack for a stick of gum. "But nobody's gonna notice anyway."

Finally, at about 4:30 p.m., a light blue pickup truck pulled into the driveway.

"That's Miguel, our gardener," Kate told me.

He drove up close to where we were sitting and hopped out of the cab. He was a small Mexican man, and the front of his jeans were stained with dirt and flecked with fresh blades of grass. He nodded to me and motioned that he was here to pick up Kate.

I brought her over and in my very worst Spanish attempted to explain to him about the bandages on her arm and what had happened with "El Gato del Gris." He listened quietly, nodding his head every now and then, and said nothing until I was finished.

"I here pick up Kate," he replied in his very best broken English. It was clear that he hadn't understood a word of what I had said.

I walked Kate around to the passenger side of the truck and asked her to please explain what happened with Lady Grey to her parents. She nodded and then reached inside her backpack again.

"I want to show you something," she said. She pulled out a Polaroid snapshot and handed it to me. "Ben took it of me and Lady Grey while you were taking pictures of the other students with their dogs. It was just before she scratched me." She shyly pulled a small Polaroid camera from her backpack and handed it over to me.

"I hope you're not too mad," she said softly.

I turned over the snapshot in my hand. There was Kate, eyes beaming, holding Lady Grey up to her cheek, happy as a girl could be.

"No, Kate," I replied, handing her back the Polaroid. "I'm not mad at all." I looked over at Miguel, who was climbing back into his truck.

"Este nina es muy especial, verdad?" ("She's a special girl, isn't she?") I asked him, touched by the little girl's bravery and determination.

Miguel smiled. His face looked nice in the late-afternoon light.

*purr*

# CHAPTER 5

# Charlotte

EMIL WENNER'S TWO-CAR garage at 15 Orchard Road was what all home workshops aspire to be. Simple and immaculate, it was a bright and cheery place, mainly because it had the one precious commodity that most of the detached garages on our block lacked: electricity.

Perfectly plumbed and paneled with white pegboard, all four walls boasted an array of carefully arranged metal hooks that cradled everything from bamboo rakes and hedge clippers to neatly coiled extension cords and fishing poles. On the wall above Emil's workbench, screwdrivers were lined up like well-trained soldiers, and weathered ball-peen hammers shared quarters with thick monkey wrenches and wiry hacksaws. A great, red vice stood bolted on the end of his workbench, its silver handle always beckoning young hands for a twirl or two. Lawn mowers gleamed in well-lit corners, and heavily bristled push brooms and dustpans hung at the ready above spotless concrete floors. It was a dream garage, the kind of setup that feeds the imagination of young boys enamored with the dangerous whine of table saws and electric drills, and many nights my brother and I would gaze out our upstairs bedroom window, trying to figure out what kind of project was taking shape beneath the cozy glow of the fluorescent shop light below.

Charlotte

Whereas Emil's garage was the model home workshop, ours was the complete opposite. Dark, damp, and dreary, it was our very own brown-shingled dungeon—a place where the domestic and the natural world collided (and the natural world always won).

Any trip to our garage was an adventure. A mother's bidding to retrieve a bag of lawn fertilizer or a cat carrier meant reaching under dusty potting tables into the deepest and darkest corners, where dozens of hungry spiders lurked inside webby hammocks, waiting patiently for the slightest vibration to leap out at bare hands and fingers. Finding a rake or garden hoe, particularly in spring, first meant you had to get past the pointed dive bombings and attacks of mother starlings on their way to the rafters to feed their young. Lowering screen windows down from those same rafters increased the possibility of a direct encounter with a horde of angry paper wasps, and oh, how earwigs loved to gather under old cans of paint and turpentine.

Every so often, armed with spray cans of Raid, buckets, brooms, and paintbrushes, we'd attempt to take back our shanghaied outpost. But in the end, even our most ambitious efforts fell short. Without electricity we were no match for the creeping vines, mice, and centipedes. Our garage would forever be ruled by living things.

For this reason it would never lose its appeal as a way station for the few brave feral cats willing to test the waters beyond the field of glass next door. It was Sweet Kitty's last stop before she joined our family.

Charlotte would be a bit bolder.

"Will someone *please* explain to me why there's cat hair all over my suitcase?" Mom exclaimed one Saturday morning. It was a good question. Sweet Kitty, who never ventured into the basement, had recently died, and Cokie had been gone for over a year.

"Ellsworth, where did you find this suitcase?" My father was just walking out the door to do his "Saturdays with Sinatra" radio show down at the station.

"Next to the furnace, Dottie," he replied.

Mom dragged the suitcase out to the backyard and started wiping it down with a damp sponge. Next door, Emil was hammering away in his perfect workshop, and his wife, Delphine, was hanging laundry.

"Hiya, Dottie."

"Good mornin', Del."

Delphine Wenner was one of my mom's best friends. She'd lived in the house next door to us for many years, first with her mother and then with her own family. Given the fact that our houses were barely twenty feet apart, it's not surprising that their relationship had its ups and downs and that at least twice a year an invisible wall of pride and stubbornness—usually born out of some benign disagreement or remark—would rise above the split-rail fence separating our two yards.

During these semiannual tiffs, all family members were forbidden to engage in any kind of conversation across the fence, and a stony silence would hang over any parallel activities in our backyards. My father and Emil would often wink at each other across the driveway; both knowing from experience that it was just a matter of time before the cold war would thaw. Their son Pete and I were best friends, and we'd always take bets at the bus stop over how long the squabbles might last.

"I give it one more week," Pete would declare.

"Not with the school-board elections coming up this Friday," I'd retort. "They'll be back at the fence by Thursday afternoon." I was usually right.

On the morning of the mysterious Cat Hair Caper, all was well on the south end of Orchard Road.

"I think there's a cat living in your basement," Delphine quipped.

"Really?" Mom responded, raising an eyebrow.

"Yes. We saw it crawl in the basement window last night as we pulled in the driveway. Scared the hell out of Emil and me. We thought Sweet Kitty had come back from the dead, except this one had a tail." My mother walked around to the side of the house. Sure enough, there was a crack in the basement window large enough for a cat to sneak through.

You can't blame Charlotte for choosing the basement over the garage. It was warm and cozy, and hardly anyone ventured into the storage space behind the paneled family room. There she could sleep most of the night, disturbed only by the lazy taps of dog paws lumbering across the oak floorboards above or the occasional whoosh of a toilet flush spiraling down thick pipes inside the walls. Surrounded by cardboard boxes filled with Christmas ornaments and stacks of old *National Geographic* magazines, the toasty den was a perfect hideout. She probably could have lived down there unnoticed for a long time if it hadn't been for a pair of headlights and an unexpected trip to Florida.

The trip my mom had to make to Florida that summer was not for a vacation. My grandfather had died, and it was my ten-year-old sister, Susan, who eventually found Charlotte in the basement. Mom was still away when she made the call.

"Del was right, Mom," Susan said. "There *is* a kitty living in the cellar. Can we keep her, *please?*" Mom took a deep breath for the obligatory "no more pets" speech.

"Absolutely not," she said, without skipping a beat. "We have no idea where she came from, your brother has just left for college, you have school coming up, your father is working, and I'm not going to be solely responsible for taking care of another animal in this house. Absolutely not!"

"But Mom," Susan argued. "She looks just like Sweet Kitty, and I've already given her a name!" (Note to kids: When lobbying parents to keep a stray animal, always tell them that you've already given it a name. Parents find that one impossible to resist.)

It's little wonder that my mom's jaw dropped when she first returned from Florida and saw Sweet Kitty's ghost curled up on the cobbler's bench. The lush bouquet of white whiskers that blossomed from Charlotte's long nose combined with the tabby black "M" emblazoned on her forehead were a perfect match, and her somewhat chubby body was identical to Sweet Kitty's. The likeness would become even more eerie a few weeks later when, just like Sweet Kitty, she'd lose her tail to a car in front of our house.

"Didn't we already do this?" the same veterinarian who had treated Sweet Kitty asked.

"Yes," my mom responded. "Twelve years ago."

I never got to know Charlotte very well. The year I left for college, Sweet Kitty passed away, and the new addition, Charlotte, took over as the feline steward of the family. Her main purpose was not to ease the fears of small boys and girls afraid of the dark but to comfort the lives of mothers and fathers adjusting to empty bedrooms and quieter kitchens.

"Never turn away a cat that shows up at your door," my mom would always say. "You never know what gifts they might bring."

Just as Sweet Kitty had done, Charlotte would become one of my mother's greatest companions and allies. Her gentle and fresh presence would help Mom through some of the longest nights of her life, sleepless nights that often come when husbands work too much and oldest sons are away at school—or when police officers call in the middle of the night.

"Mrs. Shiebler?"

"Yes?"

"Mrs. Shiebler, this is Sergeant Philbin from the East Orange police department. I'm sorry to bother you so late, but your son has been in an accident."

My mother fell to the couch. Charlotte tried to jump in her lap, but she pushed her away.

"Oh, my God, is he all right?"

"He's got a nice bump on his forehead, but he's fine. The vehicle, however, is a total loss." Charlotte knew that blue Oldsmobile well. It had originally belonged to Del and Emil next door. On nights when they came home late from bingo at St. Joseph's, she'd sleep for a few hours on the warm hood. Sergeant Philbin continued.

"Mrs. Shiebler, I just need a few minutes of your time to verify some insurance information."

My mom nodded her head and stumbled over to her beloved grandmother's cherry desk, which had been passed down to her when her grandmother died. She returned to the phone with a stack of papers, gave the officer some numbers, thanked him, and hung up. Charlotte again tried to climb into her lap, but she pushed her away.

My mother paused for a moment, got up, and walked into the dining room. She opened the top right-hand drawer of the maple hutch and reached way into the back. She grabbed something, closed the drawer, walked into the kitchen, and returned to the living room with a saucer and a pack of matches.

It had been seven years since my mother had smoked her last cigarette. She sat down in the old English rocker, slowly tapped out one of the wrinkled dowels from her secret soft pack of Newports, placed it between her lips, struck a match with her trembling fingers, and brought the flame up to its thinly papered tip. She inhaled slowly and deeply, vigorously shook out the match, and sunk back into her chair, truly believing that if there was anyone in the world that deserved a cigarette tonight, it was she. Charlotte made one last attempt to climb into my mother's lap as she picked up a half-finished crossword puzzle and a pencil off the old cobbler's bench. This time, she didn't push her away.

*purr*

# CHAPTER 6

# Quiche Lorraine

THE SNOWY MEADOWS ALONG Distillery Road passed by like a dream. The spell of freezing rain and snow that had fallen during the night had transformed even the most common works of humans and nature into displays of wonder. Glazed telephone lines sagged in between ice-covered poles, and the hemlocks and rhododendrons that framed the front steps and driveways of the many farmhouses along the road were beginning to shed their shimmering overcoats in the warm morning light. Soon we'd have to turn left, just beyond the old dairy farm. I held Quiche Lorraine in my arms in the same way I had held her some ten years before, when I found her in the parking lot of my grandmother's retirement home. It was Christmas Eve.

"Gram, let's come up with a couple of really obscure songs for charades tomorrow night," I said, grinning. She held on to my arm as we walked along the winding concrete pathway leading to her door. When we reached the porch steps, she turned to me and smiled.

"I already have one," she whispered. She grabbed hold of the railing and started making her way up the stairs.

"You do?" I asked curiously, watching her fumble around with her purse. She tilted her bag toward the porch light in hopes of finding the front-door key.

"Yes," she continued. "It's an old Billy Rose and Marty Bloom song from the early twenties. Do you think anyone will know 'Does the Spearmint Lose Its Flavor on the Bedpost Overnight?'" We both burst out laughing. A game or two of charades after Christmas dinner was a holiday tradition in our home.

"Wouldn't it be great if Phil Roll got that one?" I snickered.

"He'd have an absolute fit!" Gram exclaimed. She finally held up a faded gold key. "Found it," she said. "See you tomorrow, dear."

"Bye, Gram."

As I leaned over to kiss her good night, I felt something brush up against the back of my pant leg.

"Oh, *there* you are," Gram said calmly, looking past my legs. Standing attentively in the dim light and innocently looking up at us was one of the prettiest cats I had ever seen.

"I thought you weren't allowed to have pets here, Grandma," I said quietly.

"We're not," she said. "But she's been hanging around my front walk for almost a month, and I've been feeding her a little bit. Isn't she gorgeous?"

"Yes," I replied. "She's beautiful."

Gram continued. "The superintendent told me yesterday that he's going to call the pound after Christmas." I leaned over and scratched the side of the cat's neck. Her whole body vibrated as she purred with delight.

"She *must* belong to somebody," I said.

Gram looked at me with a twinkle in her eye. "She does belong to someone."

"Who?" I asked.

"You."

And that's how Quiche Lorraine came into my life.

Anyone who's lived in Manhattan for any length of time will tell you that city life is incomplete unless you have a great apartment cat. It also doesn't hurt to have a great apartment. At the beginning of my seven-year adventure in the Big Apple, I was lacking in both areas. My first place, a five-flight walk-up situated above a cheap seafood restaurant on the Upper East Side of Manhattan, was a dingy railroad flat, long and narrow, with ugly orange carpeting, no closets, noisy neighbors, and terrible heat. Linda, my new bride-to-be, didn't particularly care for my unimpressive bachelor pad.

"I'm sorry, but I don't think that wrapping our new vacuum cleaner in plastic garbage bags on the fire escape qualifies as a utility room," she justifiably pointed out one day during a thunderstorm. A month later we moved.

Our second apartment on the Upper West Side was a gem. A few doors down from the glorious Ansonia Hotel in a strapping prewar building, 244 East 74th Street was our first *real* home. Situated on the ninth floor with a peek-a-boo view of the Hudson River, it had two large bedrooms, a living room, a formal dining room, a good-size kitchen, and two bathrooms. It had the feel of a big old country house, and the parquet wood floors and glassed kitchen cabinets gave it a rich, homey quality. It was here that Linda and I decided to get married, which we did in the spring of 1981, beginning our long journey together.

Quiche Lorraine was named after one of our favorite B-52s songs at the time. She was also the first living addition to our new family (besides our philodendrons), and she accepted her role as a Manhattan apartment cat with grace and ease. Independent, yet kind and respectful, the sight of her sleeping on one of the long radiator boxes beneath the bank of living-room windows was the perfect welcoming mat after a long day of battling the sounds and furies of the city. She was our grounding wire, and I don't think we would have enjoyed living there as much without her calming influence each day. And there's something about reading the *New York Times* in bed on a Sunday morning with a cat curled up in the Arts and Leisure section that defines contentment. Add a cup of coffee from Zabar's and an H&H bagel, and you've got yourself a little bit of heaven on earth.

But as much as we loved living in New York City, the pace and constant hum of urban life began to eat away at our nerves and ambition. Linda and I started talking about a life outside the city and about starting a family. Even Quiche seemed to be getting a little tired and bored of the indoor life, as witnessed by her daily strolls, much to our horror, along the narrow ledge outside our ninth-floor living-room window. So after doing a little exploring, we decided to move to a small, commutable, suburban town in northern New Jersey.

Quiche really blossomed in our new suburban home. She delighted in the variety of activity outside our kitchen window, and she'd often sit for hours on the sill, chattering away at the chickadees and sparrows flitting from the bushes to the feeder. She adored the small, grassy yard behind our house, and many mornings I'd find her rolling on her back in the cool, dew-tipped lawn beneath the purple lilac bush. For the rest of the day, she'd sunbathe on the concrete steps leading up to the front porch, another one of her favorite pastimes.

A fine huntress and mouser, she was extremely proud of her skills and loved to show off her work. Many nights we'd be awakened by a strange sensation coupled with an expectant presence at the end of our bed. A groggy reach for a night-table lamp would usually reveal some kind of matted, grayish creature twitching about by our feet. Linda and I would both shriek in protest, and Quiche would quickly grab her prize and leap away. Although disappointed at our lack of attention at three in the morning, she made sure we'd eventually notice her handiwork by carefully depositing some kind of diminutive internal rodent organ in some heavily trafficked area or hallway. Many mornings I'd have to do an impromptu jig around a fresh spleen just to get to the bathroom.

She'd always return, however, and there was rarely a night when she didn't sleep by our sides. Once back on the bed, she'd stake her claim in the crook of a leg or rumple of a blanket and not move for the rest of the night. This was quite a feat considering the fact that Linda and I are somewhat restless sleepers, and on any given night our bed can resemble the North Atlantic in a blistering gale. But regardless of how many times we tossed and turned in the night, she'd always hold her position, rolling, pitching, and bobbing above our shifting bodies like a furry cork on a quilted sea. She'd weather these storms with nary a protest, and though I can't remember a moment in her life when she was aggressive or hostile, she did have one peculiar habit: She loved to attack bare feet.

As long as they stayed covered, we were safe. But if for some reason, in the middle of the night, the top sheet broke away from its bottom tucks beneath the mattress and exposed our ankle and toes, forget it. She was on them like a cougar. This explains why I often slept in the fetal position in heavy socks for the better part of six years.

When it came to grooming, Quiche was nothing short of an artist. Like a sculptress working on her own self-portrait, every twist and turn, every stroke was a study in finesse, focus, and intricate design. Eyes gently closed as if in silent meditation, she'd move up and down her body in a seamless flow, never straining or rushing. Many mornings I'd linger over breakfast to watch these elegant spruce-ups, marveling at the peace and contentment that surrounded her graceful movements and gentle stretches.

Quiche had two great loves in her life: my wife Linda and a shepherd/collie mix named Brodie.

Some of the most wonderful relationships that I've ever observed in my many years of owning and working with animals have been those between dogs and cats. When I was a boy, Sweet Kitty and my mother's cherished dachshund, Juliet, were inseparable. They were often found sleeping together in the old rocker, nestled belly to belly like a couple of well-worn loafers in a shoebox.

Quiche's connection with Brodie was just as heartwarming—a deep, affectionate bond with few bells and whistles. They never played or ran about together. No silly games, chases, or swipes from around corners. There was a quiet sophistication to their friendship, and it was clear that they just enjoyed being in each other's company.

Quiche Lorraine

So when a hunter in the woods behind our house deliberately shot off Brodie's front paw one autumn morning, their bond became forged in steel. Quiche became Brodie's twenty-four-hour on-call nurse. For three months she never left Brodie's side. Every whimper, every deep sigh was accompanied by some kind of tender gesture of concern. She'd quietly sit behind Linda and me as we changed bandages and cleansed wounds, often sealing the procedure with a few licks of her own when we were finished. Each night, she'd forfeit her usual spot on the end of our bed for a corner of Brodie's blanket beneath the pine table in the dining room. She was her faithful guardian and caretaker, and she didn't resume her normal daily routines until Brodie's leg had completely healed.

Ironically, a few months after tirelessly attending to her wounded friend, Quiche stopped eating and withdrew to a distant corner under our bed. After a visit to our local animal hospital and a thorough examination, it was determined that she had a malignant tumor.

The only time Quiche ever lost her cool was during her yearly visits to the vet. It was here that she totally fell apart. Any kind of excursion in the cat carrier reduced her to a yowling, drooling mess. That's why, on our final trip together, I left the carrier in the garage and held her in my lap.

We made the turn at the dairy farm that February morning and headed up a fairly steep hill. The islands of wet snow not yet swept aside by the village snowplows made our climb somewhat trickier, but by the time we reached the animal hospital's parking lot, we noticed it had been freshly cleared, a private rig no doubt, perhaps in exchange for a free checkup for a barn cat or a year's supply of flea shampoo.

Dr. Charles Brown's office was in a side section of a lovely white farmhouse with dark green shutters. The gray wooden steps creaked loudly as we carefully walked up them to a small, silver bell hanging from a red ribbon on the front door. It jangled cheerfully despite our heavy hearts as Linda opened it up and walked ahead of me.

We knew Quiche was very sick. We had little money. The odds were only fifty-fifty even if we could afford the operation. It was one of the most difficult decisions we had ever had to make together.

"It's the right thing to do," Dr. Brown said softly.

We stood in the waiting room together. A chickadee flew to a wooden bird feeder hanging from a long nail outside the window. I kissed Quiche on the top of her head and handed her to Linda. I then turned around and walked back outside to the car. I didn't look back.

For years I carried around the guilt of not being there for Quiche at the end. The shame and regret haunted me for a long time. *Why couldn't you have been stronger? You loved her so much; why didn't you stay? Why didn't you stay?*

Fifteen years later, I got a second chance.

Brodie had spiked a fever in the night. Those legs and hips of hers that had chased the white-tailed deer and rabbits through the fields and meadows of our farm for so many years had finally given out. There was only one thing to do.

The attending vet at the emergency clinic was an attractive young woman in her early thirties. The office was empty except for a small staff. It was Easter morning.

"I just couldn't bear to see her suffer one more night," I explained.

"It's the right thing to do," she said gently.

I held Brodie close, surrounded by a gathering of angels disguised as interns and bound by a promise I'd made to Quiche years ago about her three-legged friend. Each gave me a little bit of strength, faith, and courage and helped me lead an old girl home.

*purr*

# CHAPTER 7

# Rainbow

SHE WAS BORN ON the earthy campus of Warwick Valley Feed and Grain beneath a listing, rundown storage shed that housed the twenty-five- and forty-pound bags of grain and sweet feed we regularly purchased for the horses on our small farm. The smallest of a litter of five, she was not my four-year-old daughter's first choice. Hayden had fallen for a gray and white tabby she called Butterfly, but when we returned the following day to claim her, she had disappeared during the night, as had most of her littermates. All that remained was one very frightened and shivering kitten huddled in a dusty corner beneath that rickety shack.

Using the irresistible combination of spoons clanging against cat-food cans, we eventually coaxed the nervous kitten out of her miniature safe house, and Hayden immediately named her Rainbow, partly for her favorite movie at the time, *The Wizard of Oz*, but mostly because of the cuffs and stripes of orange, white, black, and gray that banded along her tiny frame. I tucked her into my warm coat, and with the usual assortment of new-kitten toys and "specially formulated" kitten food in the back seat of the car, we brought her home.

Convincing a child that a brand-new kitten is not a toy but an actual living, breathing animal is a very difficult task. One learns quickly in those first few weeks that it's not the training of the pet that is most

Rainbow

nerve-wracking but the training of the child. I can't imagine how many times in my life I've stopped in the middle of phone conversations to say, "Honey, don't blow in the kitten's face" or "Honey, don't pull the kitten's tail or stick your fingers in her ears" or "Honey, don't carry her around like that" or "Honey, why don't you give the kitten a rest for a little while?" And if I had a dime for every time I've said, "Honey, she's not a toy," I'd be a millionaire. That first week with Hayden and Rainbow was quite a challenge.

"What's in your purse, honey?" my wife asked Hayden one morning at breakfast.

"Rainbow, Mommy," she replied. "I'm taking her to school with me."

This particular Barbie purse was about five inches in diameter. To this day, we have no idea how she managed to stuff Rainbow in there.

Linda ran over, grabbed the purse, and unzipped the top. Like a furry jack-in-the-box, out popped the tiny, dazed head of Rainbow. Of course, we scolded her and told her never to do that again. But in the eyes of a four-year-old girl, a kitten must be the most wondrous toy imaginable!

And under such a magic spell, it's difficult to find a proper way to criticize a child's fervent desire to hug, kiss, and squeeze a kitten. Their furry presence seems to inspire an uncontrollable and boundless rush of affection and love. Even today, some seventeen years later, I have seen Hayden scoop up one of our cats, grit her teeth with passion and pained restraint, and declare, "I love him so much I want to squeeze him to death!"

When it came to Rainbow's four-legged introductions, the dogs accepted her with little fanfare. Brodie, our great suburban huntress, was too busy planning her late afternoon white-tailed-deer run to care. Squeeze sauntered over, gave her a quick sniffing over, and shot me a look that said, "She's fine, just as long as you still love me best."

Quiche Lorraine, however, was a different story. Our somewhat spoiled feline matriarch was not at all pleased by the prospect of another cat invading her pampered kingdom. She had no time for Rainbow's childish games. She was entering the autumn of her life, a time when small cans of gourmet food, undivided attention, and peace and quiet were in order, not avoiding hyperactive, mischief makers searching for playmates. She'd spend most of those first few months fending off surprise attacks from the insides of doorways and tops of tables and reminding Rainbow, via a steady dose of swats and hisses, that a tail attached to a sleeping cat, dangling from the edge of a bed, is *not* a play toy.

Nothing Quiche did seemed to diffuse Rainbow's boundless desire to recruit her as a chum. In Quiche's eyes Rainbow would forever be just a bratty, young, annoying intrusion in her life. Which was understandable. As far as kittens go, Rainbow was a holy terror, especially at night. Climbing kitchen cabinets, terrorizing the dogs, attacking lampshades, or wrestling with salt and pepper shakers, she was the night-shift kitten from hell, a nonstop bundle of noise and mischief from 10 p.m. to 4 a.m.

It was also during the midnight hour that she would share her ample musical talents. Most every night, just as we were drifting off to sleep, she'd jump up onto the piano and walk up and down the entire length of the keyboard, yowling and, I dare say, "singing." This creepy combination created the most hair-raising of lullabies, and when I'd get up to shoo her away, I fully expected to be attacked by a ghoul or get clunked on the head by the ghost of Antonín Dvořák.

One night, after a particularly spooky sonata and a series of ghastly vocalizations, I tiptoed out of bed and hid behind the piano. I watched in amazement as she ran around the living room for ten minutes, hot on the heels of absolutely nothing.

"She's having a flashback," Linda said as I returned to bed.

It was the only logical explanation. You see, when Rainbow was about four months old, we found her sitting motionless on our front porch with a bunch of empty morning-glory seedpods by her feet. Morning-glory seeds contain the same chemical compounds as LSD, We quickly realized that she was on a full-blown acid trip. When we called the vet, he said that there wasn't anything we could do except wait it out.

For the next six hours, she didn't eat, she didn't drink, and she didn't blink. Our newly crowned hippie cat just sat there, staring out over the field, occasionally listing to one side, totally oblivious to our tender pleas and outstretched hands filled with tempting plates of solid white tuna and bowls of milk. She was never the same after that.

To this day you can still hear her at three in the morning, spinning, leaping, and darting about, meowing and howling in the creepiest of tones, conversing with things that, undoubtedly, only she and Grateful Dead fans can understand.

You'd think that a cat born amid the fragrant aromas of hay, saddle soap, and alfalfa would be the ultimate outdoor/barn cat. Not so with Rainbow. She is strictly a house cat. On very rare occasions she might sneak past an open door in a noble attempt to explore the outside world, but she never ventures more than a few feet from the front stoop and is usually back inside at the first sound of a car passing by or a crow cawing overhead. If by chance the door closes behind her, she'll cry and wail like an abandoned child until someone lets her back in.

One spring afternoon, when she was about eight years old, I saw her slip out the back door. I fully expected her to return within thirty seconds. One minute passed. Two minutes. Three minutes. Five minutes went by, and she still hadn't come back. Knowing of her extraordinary lack of sensibility about the great outdoors, I determined that one of two things had happened: She had either drowned in the dogs' water bowl or she'd impaled herself on a cactus.

Just as I was getting ready to go and look for her, she reappeared in the doorway. Something was in her mouth. It was large. It was gray. It was feathery. It couldn't possibly be a bird. Rainbow only watched birds from behind the safety of window glass. In fact, she was the only cat I had ever known that was actually *afraid* of birds.

Much to my amazement, that clump of something spilling outside of Rainbow's mouth turned out to be a mourning dove. I don't know who looked more bewildered—the bird or Rainbow. The only thing I could figure was that some primeval brain synapse had fired up while she was in the backyard. Problem was, by the time she returned to the house, that tiny, instinctual flare-up had subsided, and all she had left was a face full of feathers and not a damn clue as to what to do about it.

"Rainbow!" I screamed.

She gave me a confused look, dropped the bird, and ran into the bedroom. The dove stood up, apparently unhurt, blinked twice, shook off a bunch of loose feathers and calmly waddled out the back door. When Linda came home from work, I told her the story.

"Maybe we should rename her," she suggested.

"What?" I queried.

"How about Brain-Low?'" she joked.

Hayden piped up in her defense. "Stop picking on her! She can't help it if she acts that way!" And she was right. Rainbow can't help it. But sometimes we can't help *not* making fun of her. I guess every household needs at least one crazy cat.

As nutty as she might be, when it comes to favorite scratching spots, she is fairly typical. Anything on or around Rainbow's head is fine. Under her chin, above her eyebrows, along the sides of her neck, even gentle scratches on the tips of her ears illicit dreamy eyes and soft purrs. Slide your finger down her spine, and she will arch her back in favor; run your fingers through her tail, and she'll chatter with glee.

But whatever you do, stay clear of the belly zone.

There are few exceptions to this rule, but in most cases, the rubbing or scratching of a cat's belly is like playing Russian roulette. It's the part of a cat's anatomy that's strictly reserved for the high rollers and thrill seekers, a place not for the faint of heart, where overconfident fingers and sluggish reflexes can pay a very painful price.

Throughout the years, the belly-zone guidelines for our cats have been as diverse and variable as their eating habits. Cradling Lucy in your arms and holding her as if you were preparing to give a baby a bottle would give you ten, possibly fifteen seconds of light scratches in the restricted area. After that, you were on your own. With Mitten, an index finger in the belly zone was like watching an inchworm crawl across the seductive pad of a Venus Fly Trap. It'd be just a matter of time before that limb became a finger sandwich, literally. With the burly and bear-cubbish Midnight, you made sure you bent your knees, lifted slowly and scratched both his back and belly at the same time or else a harvest of claws and jaws would close up around your hand like a giant clam.

As for Rainbow, I doubt if her cottony abdomen has ever known the touch of a human hand. Make the slightest move towards that region, and she is airborne. For most of her life, she's been a borderline lap cat at best. It's only in the past few years that she's become more relaxed and affectionate. That being said, at eighteen years young, she still seems to have plenty of surprises left to spring on her unsuspecting family. She is *far* from the perfect cat. But over the years, I have grown to love and cherish her more, judge her less, and prize her strange and quirky ways. There is, however, one glaring burden of behavior that has tested our patience and pushed our tolerance to the breaking point for over a decade.

Of all the things that my wife and I have battled over, money (or the lack thereof) is, by far and away, at the top of the list. It's followed by a distant yet formidable set of hot-button topics (family, children, work, household responsibilities, fishing), but somewhere between forgetting to put the toilet seat down and promising for a year to replace the leaky kitchen faucet, there's one question that has ignited more than its share of verbal rumbles and debates: *when was the last time you cleaned the cat box?*

It is estimated that retail sales of cat litter will soon top $1.5 billion. Head to any pet-supply superstore, and you'll be faced with a baffling assortment of clumping, nonclumping, single-cat, multiple-cat, scented, unscented, deodorized, odorless, antibacterial, paper-based, pine, peanut-shell, processed-orange-peel, earth-friendly, and dust-free formulas and confections. Litter boxes also come in a dizzying variety of sizes, depths, and styles, some of which include ventilated covers, domes, and "privacy tents." There are special litter-box mats, disposable liners, charcoal filters, and plastic or metal scoops and rakes, and you can also purchase fully automated litter boxes that are self-cleaning, self-washing, and self-flushing. And if you're looking to make a decorative statement in your home, there are litter boxes that double as planters shaped like country cottages, log cabins, and castles.

Despite all these options, there is no "perfect place" for a conventional litter box in a civilized home. It's like the crazy aunt that's locked up in the attic. Sooner or later, someone's going to notice that she's up there. Throughout the years, we've tried to hide the cat box in every conceivable room, corner, and spot imaginable. Each has its unique set of shortcomings. The main goal of litter-box placement is to keep it as fragrantly out of range as possible from potential houseguests. Master bathrooms are a logical choice because it's politely understood that they are private and off limits to visitors. But unless they are large enough to prevent it, the last thing I want to do when stepping out of a fresh shower is to feel the crunch of scattered cat litter beneath my feet. And there's something downright disagreeable about brushing my teeth at the same time one of my cats is scratching around in search of the perfect place to liberate himself or herself.

We've tried the master bedroom, once again in keeping with the goal of placing it as far from the civilized world as possible. But it seems as though the act of switching off a night-table lamp is the consummate digestive stimulant for most of our brood, and they'll often jump off the end of our bed in the fresh darkness to heed nature's call. Needless to say, this dedicated graveyard shift of pawing, digging, and excavating and its subsequent pungent results is not the dreamiest way to fall asleep.

Putting the cat box in the laundry room has never been an option for us as that is where the dogs usually sleep at night. And while the combination of the two makes for a very effective cleaning program, it's not a very attractive solution when your terrier jumps on your lap to give you a kiss in the morning.

That leaves my office, which has been the default cat-box location for the past five years or so. After a while, one becomes immune to the varying levels of air quality in the room, kind of like the way Los Angelinos have adjusted to the bubble of smog that often cloaks their city. To the outsider, both environs can be downright disgusting and unlivable. But I always look at it this way: it could be worse. I could be living next to a chicken farm. But with Rainbow's business-to-litter-box-accuracy rate dipping below 25 percent at last calculation, there isn't much difference.

"I think it might be time," Linda said one afternoon, as we were planning our move back to the country.

"How can you say that?" I protested. "Look, I know she's having a tough time regarding the box, but lately she's been better, don't you think?"

Linda didn't waiver.

"Go look at the top of the television," she replied, breezing by me into the kitchen.

I had cleaned my share of soggy hairballs from the top of our vintage RCA console TV set for years, but even I wasn't prepared for Rainbow's latest miscalculation that was slowly dripping down through the thin metal grates into the guts of our Dish Network satellite receiver.

"Lots of luck explaining to the service guy why you're returning the unit," Linda quipped. "It sure gives 'my dog ate my homework' a run for its money, don't you think?"

According to the ASPCA, one in every ten cats will have a "litter-box lapse" in his or her lifetime. A litter-box lapse? Rainbow never came close to having a "lapse" phase. She bypassed that by the time she was three years old and moved straight to the not-even-in-the-same-zip-code phase.

I have never known a cat that has struggled so much with going to the bathroom than Rainbow. We've had her checked multiple times for any infections or bladder disorders that may have been contributing to her difficulties throughout the years. Nothing ever came up. Personally, I think it has something to do with the morning-glory-seed incident. For as long as I can remember, she has had cat box "issues." I have watched her climb inside dozens of times, totally oblivious to her position, and with her backside hanging well over the edge, confidently miss the box completely. I used to think it was a sharing or cleanliness problem until one day, after diligently scrubbing and removing any residual evidence of other occupants and filling the plastic pan with fresh litter, she promptly jumped inside and hosed down the wall.

It has been one of the most frustrating and maddening aspects of our life with Rainbow. And when we started to look for a new place to live in the high country, the question kept coming up over and over again: what were we going to do with Rainbow?

Our plan was to rent or lease a house for a year to see if we liked the more extreme and rugged climate and lifestyle of the high desert. Many of the initial homes we looked at were newer, with fresh wall-to-wall carpeting throughout, which was problematic not only for Rainbow but for our messy indoor/outdoor dogs as well.

As so often happens when you think you've exhausted all possibilities and you're ready to call it quits, the perfect opportunity reveals itself. Such was the case one late, gray afternoon after an exhausting and fruitless search for houses, when we took "one last spin" around a neighborhood we really liked. A couple of miles in, we saw a very small FOR RENT sign that we had apparently missed on previous drive-bys, tacked to the front door of a modest house at the top of a small hill. We decided to pull over and walk up the partially washed-out driveway to get a better look.

The house seemed solid enough, and there was plenty of land to pasture our horses. I wrote down the contact number on the back of an old gasoline receipt and walked around back to check out the rest of the property. There, next to a small fenced yard off the kitchen, was the answer to all of our worries about Rainbow—a detached garage. When I peeked in the window and saw the twenty-by-twenty-foot concrete floor, I knew we had hit the litter-box mother lode.

"Honey, come here—you gotta see this!" I yelled.

Linda walked around the corner, and the moment she saw the garage, her face lit up.

"Rainbow . . . " she whispered.

Now when most people see a garage, they think of things like parking a car, storing bicycles and lawn mowers, maybe setting up a workshop and the like. Not us. With electricity, insulated windows and the washable concrete floor, all we saw an assisted-living facility and retirement home for our little old cat with the big incontinence problem. It was the perfect setup, and a month later we moved in.

On the surface, it might seem cruel to exile an aging cat to the garage. But in many ways, having been born and imprinted for the first eight weeks of her life in the most rustic of feed stores, once settled in, she seemed more than comfortable in her new country digs, the aromatic bags of grain, hay bales, and leather saddles only adding to the atmosphere of familiarity. Using cardboard boxes and plastic storage tubs freshly arranged from our move, I set about to construct a series of comfortable sleeping and resting spots, strategically placing each at different heights and levels for easy maneuverability and access. Some I draped in soft, faded beach towels; others I carefully molded and cushioned into cozy nests using old house blankets. Of course, after I had spent hours diligently designing her new living quarters, she promptly curled up on a dirty, barren plastic container filled with old garden tools.

On the third day in her new digs, the cat that hadn't swatted a fly for the better part of ten years caught a mouse. I found the trembling ball of gray huddled motionless in a lumpy corner of one of her blankets, its head buried in its tiny breast, most likely hiding out of shame and embarrassment rather than from fear or injury. I picked him up and gently placed his tiny form on a patio chair on the deck beneath an old T-shirt, where he could, hopefully, pull himself together under the warm morning sun. I came back to check on him a couple of hours later, and he was gone.

Two weeks later, in another amazing behavioral anomaly, the cat that hadn't as much as strayed an inch from her daily route between the top of the television set and her blanket on the couch (a grand total of eight and a half feet) decided one night to leave the nursing home and explore the nearly impassable chaparral behind our new house. Up to that point, her boldest move beyond the garage had been to poke her head out the door, sniff around a bit, and then dart back inside. But on this particular night, she waltzed right past me as I was bringing her dinner, trotted confidently to the inside edge of the picket fence, which she easily slipped beneath, and then, inexplicably, disappeared into the thick brush.

"Rainbow! No!" I screamed.

Knowing the danger, I ran as fast as I could, cat dish in hand, and lunged for the gate. In the process, I deftly stepped into a gopher hole and fell ass over teakettle into a pile of fresh rabbit droppings beside the concrete walkway. I stumbled to my feet, cursing my clumsiness, and made a snap decision to rush out to my truck to get a flashlight, as I was losing valuable daylight by the minute. I could already hear the feral yips of the coyotes welcoming the night throughout the valley and knew that if she got any deeper into that hillside, I would never find her.

I yelled for Linda through the open screen windows to grab a flashlight and come outside, and for one brutal hour we scoured every inch of that hillside, occasionally pausing in hopes of hearing the slightest rustle or meow in the growing darkness. We called and called, clanged spoons against favorite food dishes, even drove the car up to the edge of the thorny vegetation to scan the area with headlights and high beams. She had completely disappeared.

There always seems to come a point with me, particularly when it involves losing a pet, where resignation attaches itself to rationalization to form a temporary emotional balm. As we searched, I pitched a bulletproof, cosmic explanation for Rainbow's disappearance to Linda.

"You know," I said, while bending back the branches on a large mound of scrub oak, "the way she rushed up into those hills, it was like she was on a mission and it was *time*. Maybe she was just heeding a wild call to die in the arms of Mother Nature."

Linda shot me a look that said *that's the dumbest thing I've ever heard* and walked down toward the road. Our calls continued to go unanswered, and our hopes began to diminish even more quickly.

"It might be a good idea to drive down to the corner one more time," she said softly.

"Maybe Smokey can help," I replied, completely ignoring her suggestion.

I ran into the house and recruited our three-year-old border collie and led him up the hill.

"Where's Rainbow, Smokey? Where is she? Where's Rainbow?" I sang sweetly, hoping he would grab the scent of her trail with the same fervor he'd often display herding her between the television and the couch at the old house. But it was not to be.

"All right, boy, get up," I said, opening the car door and realizing I was asking a herding animal to magically turn into a bloodhound. Besides, it was getting dangerous out there for him as well.

I saw Linda's down-turned flashlight bobbing dejectedly up the steps of the front porch as I started the car. Rainbow was lost, and there wasn't anything more we could do about it. I felt hopeless and scared as I swung out of the driveway to try one more pass down the ever-darkening dirt road.

Suddenly, as I rounded the corner just beyond our driveway, I saw a small, dark figure standing in the middle of the road. It was Rainbow. I slammed the car into park and jumped out, trying not to spook her any more than she was. I approached her steadily and spoke to her firmly.

"What the hell are you doing, you nut case?" I said through racing heartbeats and deep breaths of relief. I slowly leaned down to pick her up. Cradling her in my left arm, I got back in the car and drove up the driveway, not quite believing who or what I was holding. Smokey leaned over my shoulder to investigate.

"She's back, Smokey," I said. "She's back."

I pulled up to the garage and carefully climbed out so as not to disturb my fragile package, now purring quite contentedly against my chest. I opened the garage door and gently let her down on the floor. She promptly jumped up to her feeding station and immediately started chowing down on a bowl of her favorite entree, Chicken and Tuna Supreme. Only then did I realize that Linda and I hadn't been dealing with some kind of impulsive, terminal vision quest. No, it was something much more along the lines of senile Aunt Martha sneaking out of the nursing home at one o'clock in the morning to score a pack of smokes down at the local convenience store. I was beyond happy to have her back home.

Later that night, I made myself a cup of tea and headed out to the garage to check on her one more time. The glow from the hanging lamp over her small bed looked warm and inviting through the big bay window, and once inside I could see that she was curled up tight underneath the makeshift heater, the 75-watt bulb giving off just enough warmth to take the edge off the cool summer night. As I quietly unfolded an old blue chaise lounge next to her, I noticed a couple of wet spots in the middle of the concrete floor. They'd be easy to clean with a damp mop and a little Clorox in the morning.

As I lowered myself down into the creaky chaise and adjusted the angle of the headrest, Rainbow's little apple head bobbed up, and she promptly jumped into my lap. As she slowly nestled down into the folds of my shirt, her gentle, wise purr began to roll soothingly across my chest. Soon she would fall asleep, and it would be hard for me not to do the same. My cup of tea was on the table by the door, but I didn't care. I'd found the perfect tonic and wasn't moving an inch.

*purr*

# CHAPTER 8

# Rosemary

THERE WAS ONLY ONE reason why kids came to the summer program at the Helen Woodward Animal Center.

"Oh, Mr. Shiebler, can we go see the dogs and cats? *Please!*" they'd beg, even before we'd reached the classroom on the first day.

As hard as the education department tried to promote a program that featured a wide assortment of animal-based activities, crafts, and projects, the students had their minds set on one thing—going to the dog kennels and the cattery as soon as possible. I fought with the powers that be on this issue quite often, and I frequently chose to exchange classroom time for extended sessions with the animals. I strongly believed that there was no better place for kids to learn about pet responsibility, compassion, and care than by taking them out to the very heart of the matter. I wanted them to climb into the lives of those orphans, to truly feel what it was like to live on those cold, concrete floors and in those metal cages. And by having that firsthand experience, I *knew* that there would be little chance any of them would be dropping off cats in cardboard boxes in the middle of the night on the front steps of the local animal shelter anytime in the future.

Which is exactly how Rosemary was brought to us.

Of all the cats that captured our hearts that summer, Rosemary was the most special. She had been found sitting in a dirty blue cat carrier on

**Rosemary**

the front steps of the center one Monday morning. She was a filthy mess of fleas and neglect, and the tight, thin collar that bore the faded letters of her name had formed a permanent scar around her neck. Her thick black-and-white coat was a nightmare of mats and tangles. But despite her condition, she purred at the first touch and the faintest sliver of attention.

Once cleaned up and given a sunny home in the cattery, she became a favorite of students, always willing to be held and stroked, never protesting a snapshot or an extra few minutes in an eager child's lap. On afternoons when we'd head out to the cattery, we'd usually find her curled up and asleep in her cozy wicker bed, and upon hearing the first jostles of her door latch, she'd calmly stand up, stretch, and heave a hearty yawn. And for the rest of the day, she'd soak up all the love and attention she could get and, in return, give the children everything they'd hoped for during their week at the center—boundless affection and tons of purrs.

I'm happy to say that soon thereafter a delightful woman who recognized this remarkably resilient cat's ability to brighten people's days adopted Rosemary. As a result, they both became very active in the local pet-therapy program, visiting hospitals and nursing homes, much to the delight and comfort, I'm sure, of their oftentimes lonely and forgotten residents. Such is the power of purrs.

It's hard to imagine, after spending time with Rosemary, how anyone could proudly define themselves "cat haters." I recently queried a number of people who could easily fit into this category, simply because I was curious to find out the reasons behind their disdain for these often misunderstood creatures. Many of their responses were the same:

"I just don't like them."

"I had a bad experience when I was a child."

"Too much hair. And besides, I'm allergic."

"They're not friendly."

"I don't like their attitude. I don't trust them."

"I'm afraid that they're going to bite or scratch me."

By far and away, the greatest concern amongst professed cat haters and ailurophobes (people who are afraid of cats) is the biting and scratching issue. And while I've fallen victim to the occasional unintentional scratch or claw mark, usually the result of a frightened or sudden leap from my lap or an acrobatic jump from a bookcase to my bare shoulders, most of the scratches, claw marks, or bites I've received throughout the years have had little to do with cats. In fact, most of the pet-related scars on my legs and arms have come from unclipped and unruly dog toenails rather than from angry cat claws. Thankfully, by using common sense and education and having a bit of old fashioned luck, I've never been seriously attacked or bitten by a dog.

Frankly, I've had more trouble with the bird family than with cats. Jimmy, our pet parakeet, would gladly take off my pinky if given the chance. And once, when I was a young teenager, while riding my bicycle to the radio station, the biggest crow I had ever seen decided to attack me. To escape, I raced up a driveway and into the garage of a complete stranger, an elderly man who was quietly working on a ship in a bottle.

"Mister," I said breathlessly, "there's a big crow out there that's trying to kill me!"

He set down his screwdriver and looked up at me through his thick, magnifying-type glasses.

"Oh, that's just Barney," he replied calmly. "He can get pretty aggressive when he's hungry." It was a pretty lame explanation for a thirteen-year-old boy who had just seen his life flash before his soon-to-be-pecked-out eyes.

And yes, I've been bitten and kicked by—and thrown off—plenty of horses. But never once have I been deliberately attacked, scratched, or bitten without provocation by any cat I've owned. The same is true with all of my friends' cats that I've come in contact with throughout the years—with one notable exception.

Linda and I had been invited to a Christmas party at a friend's apartment on the Lower East Side in New York City. It was your typical holiday gathering, with lots of fruitcake, eggnog, and people we didn't know, and I really wasn't too thrilled about attending. Besides, it was Friday, their place was way the hell downtown, and I was tired after a long week. I'd also been battling some kind of stomach bug that had been going around. But this friend was also a business acquaintance, and it was clearly one of those we-have-to-go situations.

Not long after we arrived, I began to feel some "gastrointestinal distress." So I snuck off to the lone guest bathroom that was only few feet down the hall from the living room. This was not a very large apartment, and with fifty or so guests crammed into every nook and corner, the bathroom was not the most comfortable or private place to excuse yourself to even if you were feeling perfectly fine.

I closed and locked the door behind me and took a seat. The room was decorated nicely for the holidays with festive snowman hand towels and a fresh, fragrant evergreen garland pleasantly hung around the medicine cabinet and adjoining shelves. There was even a can of "Christmas Potpourri" air-deodorizing spray on the back of the toilet.

Of course, I hadn't been in the bathroom for more than thirty seconds before the onslaught of impatient hands began turning and twisting the locked doorknob, making me feel even that much more pressured and ill at ease.

Suddenly, I heard a strange rustling sound from behind the shower curtain. I also noticed a ghostly ripple that was slowly migrating down the entire length of the fabric. I looked around for possible drafts, but without any windows or visible vents in the room, I surmised that a rogue breeze couldn't be the source of the noise. There was only one possible explanation: somebody I knew was playing a holiday prank.

"All right, c'mon out, you got me," I said nervously. There was no answer. I heard another faint rustle and saw a little more movement from behind the curtain.

"Tony, if that's you, you're a dead—" I started to say. But before I could utter another word, the shower curtain ripped violently to one side and something very large and furry landed squarely on my half-naked thighs. I looked down, and there, staring at me with two crazy, crossed eyes was what looked to be a seriously agitated Siamese cat. She then dug her claws into both of my legs, gave me a healthy swipe across the tip of my nose, and, using my bare lap as a springboard, launched herself back into the bathtub, disappearing behind the holiday shower curtain.

I staggered to my feet, thighs bleeding generously, pulled up my pants, and threw myself out the bathroom door, much to the surprise of a dozen or so guests gathered around the punch bowl down the hall.

"What the hell is going on in there?" I yelled while struggling to tuck in my shirt. The hosts of the party appeared from around the corner.

"What happened to you?" they both asked simultaneously.

"Some *thing* jumped out from behind the shower curtain and attacked me," I said breathlessly. There was a brief pause, and then suddenly the entire room burst into laughter.

"Looks like we've got ourselves a winner!" a voice yelled out from the back of the living room.

"Welcome to the club!" a tall, sophisticated woman announced, as the rest of the guests roared.

"Chloe racks up another one," a man said while slapping me on the shoulder and heading over to the bar to freshen up his drink. At that point one of the hosts came up to me.

"I totally forgot to warn you about Chloe," she said. "Are you all right?"

I nodded, still somewhat in shock. I didn't think it was worth telling her about the new set of claw marks running down the upper half of my legs.

"I'm really sorry," she continued. "You know how those Siamese cats can be."

No, actually, I didn't until *that* little episode. Last time I checked, attacking half-naked people from behind shower curtains wasn't part of the Siamese profile. Granted, Chloe's behavior was a bit bizarre, to say the least, and fertile fodder for any cat hater, but it was the reaction of the owners and guests that interested me the most. There was a certain amount of muted glee and pride from the hosts and the other guests regarding the monster cat's bathtub ambush. Frankly, despite their profuse apologies and sympathetic smiles, I highly doubted any of them really felt that bad. I was now an exclusive member of the "I Got Attacked by Chloe Club," but I couldn't quite figure out who should take the rap, Chloe or her owners.

I had my notions. A few weeks after the Christmas party, I ran into an old college friend at a restaurant. We talked for a while, and he asked me what I'd been up to lately. I told him I was writing a book about cats.

"I hate cats," he immediately replied. "They're selfish, sneaky, and can't be trusted."

With the incident still fresh in my mind, I was going to tell him all about my recent encounter with Chloe—but I quickly stopped myself. Instead, I decided to bring up the story of a cat named Rosemary.

*purr*

CHAPTER 9

Mitten

I'VE NEVER SEEN MY father cry. But I heard him once.

It was a gorgeous day in the middle of February. It had been a very mild winter, and the yellow whips of the forsythia at the top of our driveway were threatening to bloom early. The buds on the grand old sugar maple in the front yard were also beginning to swell a bit, and in a few weeks they too would feather forth another faithful spring offering of tender leaves and seeds. I had just turned eleven, and I was very happy that our school district was having budget problems. Split sessions had been deemed the temporary solution, and as a result I was walking home from the bus stop at twelve-thirty in the afternoon instead of three.

The warm day had inspired my mom to begin spring cleaning ahead of schedule, and the bank of front windows above the naked branches of the azaleas were wide open, their airy mouths filled with the lacy fringes of freshly washed curtains, beckoning me home on the breeze. A bologna sandwich would be waiting for me on the dining room table, and I'd be warned to take my shoes off in the front hall.

"No shoes! The living-room floor has just been lemon-oiled!" she'd always yell.

But something was different that day. The blue Bel Air station wagon was parked in the driveway. Dad must be home. And when I opened the screen door, Mom didn't say anything about my shoes. I took them off anyway, walked into the living room, and dropped my book bag next to the cobbler's bench. Sweet Kitty was sleeping in her usual spot, and Rusty was resting on a rug in front of the fireplace. I saw my mother sitting at the dining-room table. It was obvious that she'd been crying.

"What's the matter, Mom?" I asked. "Why is Dad home?"

I heard a door gently close in the hallway. Mom spoke in soft tones.

"It's just a very sad day, Gary," she whispered. "A very sad day."

My mother and father loved Nat King Cole. Many nights I'd fall asleep to "Mona Lisa," "Unforgettable," or "Nature Boy" playing on the big stereo console downstairs in the living room.

*"The greatest thing you'll ever learn*
*is just to love and be loved in return . . ."*

"The best ever," my Dad would always say.

So when the news of his death came over the Associated Press wire at the radio station, my father immediately left work and came home.

I stood outside the bathroom door for a long time. There is something very confusing about hearing your father cry for the first time. I was frightened. I didn't know what to say. I just stood there and listened. His sobs were strong and deep. When I finally called to him outside the door, everything got very quiet. I heard the faucet run, the towel rack jiggle, and I stepped back as the lock clicked back inside the door. When he walked out, I wanted to see his face. But he wouldn't let me.

"Hi, pal," he said weakly as he walked toward the bedroom. There was a slump in his shoulders that I'd never seen before.

"Lunch is ready," Mom called.

But I suddenly wasn't very hungry that day.

There comes a time in everyone's life when you're faced with a moment of temptation *so* strong that you're powerless to resist. A seduction so potent that regardless of how many times you might have escaped in the past, no matter how hard you try, you won't be able to say no. More dangerous than Girl Scout cookies (particularly the chocolate mint wafers) or those warm cinnamon buns with the cream-cheese icing at the county fair. I'm talking about, of course, the cardboard box of kittens in front of your local grocery store.

Such was the beginning of my life with Mitten, the cat I'd measure all others against. When Hayden was three years old, she picked her out one Saturday afternoon, in front of a supermarket, in a banana box filled with four tabbies and an orange and white calico. She let go of my hand and dipped her fingers into the box and scooped out the equivalent of a curled-up creamsicle with fur.

"Can we keep her, Daddy?" she beamed, looking up at me with hopeful eyes.

You know the rest.

WEBSTER'S DICTIONARY PARTIALLY DEFINES the word "hero" as "a mythological or legendary figure often of divine descent, a man admired for his achievements and courage."

I've had many heroes in my life. As a boy I looked to my father and the baseball players we shared together for guidance and inspiration. Mickey Mantle and my father were the undisputed heroes of my youth. That is, when it came to human beings.

Webster's continues on to say that a hero may be one "that shows great courage, the principal of an event or period, an object of extreme admiration and devotion." And that is where one illustrious and noble feline—a cat that I have always referred to as "the guy I want to be like when I grow up"—comes into play. Like many of us who have owned multiple cats throughout our lives, there is always one that takes a special place in our hearts and memories. My once-in-a-lifetime cat was Mitten.

Don't let the name fool you. This was by no means a meek, woolly, and insulated house cat, as his handle might infer. Not a chance. He was

Mitten

by far the coolest cat I have ever known. He was my hero cat, the James Bond of our animal enclave, a swashbuckling stud who handled every turn in life with an unshakable confidence and swagger. He was the man every woman dreams of—handsome, sensitive, courageous, and a little rebellious. His remarkably good-looking face boasted high cheekbones and a finely sculpted nose. A trio of well-defined chestnut stripes blazed down his forehead and eventually dissolved into a sexy, amber mask that framed his dazzling yellow eyes. His coat was hearty and thick—a rich landscape of ivory, orange, and tan. His chest was brilliant white, its tuxedoed splendor shirttailing down to his belly and eventually coating all four of his long legs in a furry snow. On the tip of his pink nose, he sported a ruddy birthmark, the kind of minor imperfection that only made him more appealing, and the various assortments of cuts and nicks he boasted on any given day only added to his roughhouse mystique and rugged charm. And because of his shared duties as indoor lap cat and backyard sheriff, his personal grooming requirements were perfunctory, no-frills affairs, nothing more than the occasional "cowboy bath on the range." His strategic oversights of driveway motor-oil swatches or patches of dirt were important signatures, reminding us that no matter how many nights he curled up inside the folds of our soft, flannel sheets, he was still a tough guy at heart.

Mitten's purr was like a Harley Davidson idling at a stoplight, powerful and loud, and he walked the floors and counters of our house like a whiskered Clark Gable. One wondered how anyone or anything could carry himself with such certitude and aplomb. But in spite of all these virile qualities, he did have one significant flaw.

He couldn't meow.

Imagine Popeye as a baby with an upper respiratory infection or a baby chimp with laryngitis. A descending cadence of scratchy cracks and squeaks, it was the one chink in his armor—his vulnerable spot. It did little to offset his intrepid demeanor and invincible air. It was just another lovable and endearing part of this gallant and gutsy cat.

Despite Mitten's bravado and macho facade, he had no problem, as my wife put it, with getting in touch with his "feminine side"—particularly when it came to playing with our daughter, Hayden. Whereas Rainbow was barely tolerant of Hayden's attempts to enlist her as a little sister, Mitten was always cooperative and open-minded, never too busy to pass up a ride in a plastic shopping cart or to play dress up. Each day after kindergarten, Hayden would scoop him up off the windowsill and plop him in the cart, where he'd sit patiently as Hayden gathered dolls and tucked various toys around him. Then, nestled on a cozy throne of blankets and pillows, he'd calmly ride from room to room, eyes at half mast, purring contentedly, paws tucked neatly beneath his chest, like a holy man in a rickshaw being escorted to the royal palace. When the ride was over, he'd calmly stand up, stretch, yawn, and return to the windowsill until called upon for another excursion.

Fashion shows were also a weekly event, and Mitten was always first call for any modeling assignments. Dresses, hats, jumpers, bloomers, pajamas, T-shirts and short sets—Mitten willingly wore them all. Whether it be sprawled out on the end of a bedspread posing in the latest evening wear or sitting on a white wicker couch showing off a snappy spring outfit, he'd patiently sit for frame upon frame, always game and fully tolerant of Hayden's learning curve with the Instamatic. I have never known a cat so willing to please a child. I will forever be grateful to him for the hours and hours he so lovingly devoted to the happiness of my little girl.

Ironically, for the first year of his life, we thought John Wayne was a female. We only realized our error when we took Mitten to the vet to get spayed. Later that afternoon, we got a call from the office.

"Mr. Shiebler?"

"Yes?"

"This is Sandy from Dr. Brown's office. We seem to have a problem regarding the spaying."

As I usually do with all of my pets, I immediately shifted into worst-case-scenario mode, probably from watching too many episodes of *ER*. They had probably found a tumor—it was cancerous, and I was going to have to make a decision at that very moment whether or not I was willing to spend the fifteen hundred dollars to have the operation. Of course, we didn't have the money, but it was Hayden's favorite cat in the whole world. What was I going to do?

"Mr. Shiebler?"

"Yes, I'm still here. What's the problem?"

I steadied myself against the fateful diagnosis.

"Well, Mr. Shiebler. Mitten isn't a she, he's a he."

I thought of how perfectly stunning Mitten had looked that morning in that pastel pink cotton jumper and laughed. We broke the news to Hayden gently. She didn't take it well.

"I don't want her to be a him," she wailed. "I want him to be a she!"

For years, I still stayed mixed up.

"Dad, where's Mitten?" Hayden would ask.

"I haven't seen her," I'd reply.

"Him, Dad, not her." Eleven-year-old daughters *love* to correct their fathers.

When it comes to food, I have known many cats with unusual appetites. A student of mine at the shelter once claimed that she had a cat that loved to eat corn on the cob. I broke it to her gently that there was no way a cat would eat corn on the cob unless it were on the verge of starvation. The next day, she returned to class, proof in hand. That morning my entire fifth-grade class was treated to a fifteen-minute video titled, "Edgar: The Corn on the Cob Cat." I never questioned her claims again.

Mitten's palate was equally adventurous. Unlike Rainbow and our latest fussbudget, Clementine, Mitten was always game to try something new. A real meat-and-potatoes kind of guy, he'd eat just about anything. He adored Saltine crackers and frequently helped himself to party trays and cheese boards at holiday time. Of course, you never turned your back on him while making a tuna or chicken salad sandwich. And if the phone rang while you were eating a bowl of cereal, you didn't dare answer it. And it was always a good idea to be a little extra careful when you treated yourself to a French toast breakfast on Sunday morning. Drop your napkin on the floor, and you may sit up to find a cat lapping up your maple syrup.

He was a great explorer, a tireless snooper, and any combination of empty boxes, dresser drawers, linen closets, cabinets, or bookshelves was fair game for a potential playground or nest. Many nights, in the usually benign act of retrieving a pot or pan to make dinner, I'd be scared half to death by an orange and white blur leaping from a kitchen cabinet or pantry. His insatiable appetite for adventure, both indoors and out, was always a source of concern for us, as he was the master of close calls, leading me to believe that he did not glean any wisdom from death-defying experiences.

"That's why cats need nine lives," Linda would always say.

Mitten was the perfect example of a cat that needed every life he could get his paws on. Once he spent three weeks with a plastic bell on his head and abscess-draining tubes sticking out of his side after a late-night battle with a couple of backcountry feral cats behind our garage.

Two days after the bell came off and the stitches were removed, he was scratching to go out again.

Another night, at about three in the morning, Linda and I were awakened by the sound of a mysterious clanging coming from our front porch, a sound that could only be described as an impromptu solicitation from Dickens's Ghost of Christmas Past. We opened the door, and to our horror there was Mitten, with a toothy animal trap clamped shut on his right front paw. I managed to pry it free, and after a frantic trip to the all-night animal clinic, it was determined that the trap had miraculously closed between the joints on his paw and he'd be fine in the morning.

"He must have gotten it snagged somewhere down in the canyon," I said to Linda as we were driving home. "I can't imagine him dragging that thing all the way back to the house. Maybe he's learned his lesson this time."

No such luck.

The next night, as I was going outside to change a lightbulb on the front porch, he bolted through my legs before I could close the door to block him. I gave chase but to no avail. He jumped over the fence and disappeared back down into the canyon.

I will say this: the year we lived in the mountains, Mitten became a little more hesitant about going outdoors. Perhaps he sensed a more potent danger in the unforgiving hills that surrounded our farm. Maybe the wild wails of the coyote or the scream of the red-tailed hawk soaring above the jagged peaks of the Cuyamaca range convinced him to stay a little closer to home. Perhaps it was the majesty of the massive Coulter pines or the fierce Santa Ana winds blowing up from the Anza Borrego desert that told him that the rules were different there. Or maybe he simply understood that he wasn't as fast and invincible as he used to be. Still, he would always be drawn to the outdoors and forever be curious about the wilder things in life. And he will always be the greatest cat I've ever known.

That change came slowly and mysteriously. At first, I thought that both Mitten's eyesight and hearing might be failing a bit due to old age, but when he started wandering about aimlessly, oftentimes getting stuck in closet and pantry corners that he used to negotiate so easily, I knew something was very wrong. And when he started to miss the cat box, a behavior unheard of from this proud and dignified cat, I decided to take him to the vet.

I had heard about feline AIDS and its symptoms that included restlessness, disorientation, and incontinence but wasn't ready to accept that incurable diagnosis, even though I knew in my heart that's what it was. I thought of the many fights Mitten had waged with the feral cats that invaded our property every night, and I was convinced that's how he'd been infected. I felt deeply guilty for not protecting him better, for not trying to keep him inside more, even though I knew that things like rolling in the dirt and greeting Linda in the driveway every evening as she opened her car door were more important than keeping him locked up behind steel screen doors.

There's a scene in the film *The Horse Whisperer* where Robert Redford's character, a tough, independent rancher and horse trainer, is asked what he fears most about getting older.

"Not being much use to anyone or anything anymore," he responds.

It may seem a bit foolish to apply that same sentiment to Mitten's wishes regarding getting older, but if there's one thing I believe in with all my heart, it's that he deserved to move on with dignity and respect. I couldn't stand to see what he was becoming, and I have to believe that he would have felt the same way, too.

It would be our decision as to when we wanted to let him go. On the afternoon before we took him to the hospital, I was lying on the couch getting ready to take a nap— something we always did together—when just like the old days, he jumped up into my lap and slowly lowered himself down onto my chest. He began to purr softly and reassuringly, and for a few precious minutes he was back in the world with me. He had come to say goodbye, and it was almost too much to bear. But like hundreds of times before, he helped me through the tears and pain just by the simple act of being there. Sometimes, that's all it takes, just being there.

We drifted off together that afternoon, and I dreamed about my father and the day Nat King Cole died. I called him the following morning.

"Do you have any extra albums you could send me?" I asked.

My father seemed pleasantly surprised by my request.

"I've got doubles of most everything Nat's recorded." he said "I'll put together a bunch of great stuff for you, OK?"

"Don't forget 'Unforgettable,'" I said.

"I won't, pal," he said. "I won't."

*purr*

# Wyatt and Doc

WHEN IT COMES TO tough kids, tough dogs, and tough cats, I enjoy working with them all. I certainly had my share of each while teaching at the shelter—Lady Grey, Kate, Frazier, Brandon, Cherokee, Carter, and a host of others. I approached them all the same: with patience, as much consistency as I could muster, and a hell of a lot of imagination.

One of the challenges I faced with students that had chosen cats as opposed to dogs for their weekly adoptions was whether or not the cats would pay any measurable attention to their starry-eyed admirers. Knowing how withdrawn shelter cats can be, particularly if you compare them to the more outgoing and entertaining dogs housed outside in the kennels, I was concerned that the cat kids would get bored over time with the more reserved and less active clan of felines that lived in the cattery.

Surprisingly, many students were perfectly content to just sit and peer through the white-wired gates of their enclosures, happy to see the slightest acknowledgement of their presence, and downright thrilled if their cats actually approached them for a passing rub against their extended fingers. It proved that my mom was right when she said that "dogs are like coffee, and cats are like tea" and to see how content and patient the cat devotees were with their oftentimes timid and shy selections was a testament to her wisdom.

"Mr. Shiebler, she looked at me! She likes me!" students would often proclaim proudly in the cattery, so appreciative of the smallest tidbit of attention that might be directed their way. It reinforced my belief that less is more when it comes to getting to know a cat and that one must be satisfied with the smallest revelations when it comes to the disclosure of a cat's temperament or personality. You also have to slow down. As with a cup of tea, it's hard to appreciate the subtle flavor and pleasure of the brew if you're jogging around the reservoir in Central Park while text messaging the office. That's why we have dogs and coffee.

At the beginning of the week, depending on the advice of the kennel techs as to who was approachable and whom I should avoid, I'd make a list of the more friendly and personable cats in the cattery that the kids could safely adopt for the week. On the first day I'd take them on a walk-through so they could make their choices. I'd also announce that I'd be letting a select group of cats out of their cages so they could mingle with the class. This always brought a flurry of chatter and glee from the students until I explained that on the first day there would be no physical contact.

"Today you are aspiring behavioral scientists," I'd explain. "Each of you will receive a pad and pencil, and you'll write down observations of your cats' behaviors. There will be no verbal or physical contact initiated by you whatsoever."

"But Mr. Shiebler," they'd protest. "Can't we pick them up?"

"Let me ask you this," I'd say. "How would you feel if somebody you just met reached down and picked you up without asking?"

"If I was a cat," blurted out a restless but likable kid named Carter, "I'd scratch him!" Many of his fellow students nodded their heads in agreement.

"Don't you think that some of the cats in here today might feel the same way if you did that?" I asked.

The room got very quiet. I could hear their little brains whirring and processing the information that I had just shared. I love those moments when kids truly *get it,* especially when it comes to respecting and caring for their pets.

So on that first day, I sat them down in the middle of the cattery floor and carefully let each "subject" out of its cage, reminding the students that no matter how tortuous it might be they were only allowed to observe and not touch. It was hilarious to see the pleading faces on the kids who fell victim to the more amorous and affectionate cats that would rub up against them or even curl up by their feet.

"Today you are impartial social scientists!" I'd bellow, secretly grateful that I didn't have to participate in the exercise. But it was a valuable lesson, demonstrated by their responses to my questions later on in the classroom.

"So how did that go?" I asked casually.

"It was torture, Mr. Shiebler!" they'd all laugh and scream. "You are so mean!"

"So what did you learn about your cats, my little scientists?" I continued.

"I learned that Flower likes to walk around and sniff everything," one girl said.

"And that Smoke doesn't like other cats," another added.

"Wyatt and Doc didn't even come out of their cage!" Carter yelled.

"My cat came over and started playing with my shoelaces right away," a girl named Chelsea said proudly.

"And you wouldn't have learned any of these things about your cats if I'd let you just run in there, open their cages, and pick them up, right?" I asked. A cooperative sigh of acceptance and agreement resonated throughout the classroom.

"But, Mr. Shiebler, when can we hold them?"

"Tomorrow," I promised the very patient and endearing group of fifth and sixth graders.

The following day, armed with feathers, balls of yarn, and an assortment of kitty toys, we all headed down to the cattery. Once again,

Wyatt

I asked the students to sit down in a circle in the middle of the soft-carpeted floor, and one by one I opened the doors to the cat condos. Within minutes, a flood of furry and not-as-bashful occupants began to spill out of their cubicles, obviously quite comfortable with the surroundings and its guests, aided, no doubt, by our understated and low-key visit the day before.

"Looks like an organized prison break," I chuckled to one of the vet techs.

From the looks on the children's faces, you would have thought it was Christmas morning and they'd received every present on their wish list. For the next twenty minutes, they showered their temporarily adopted orphans with as much love and attention as any living thing could hope for. And much to the delight of an awkward kid named Carter, even his shy selections for the week, Wyatt and Doc, had wandered cautiously out of their cozy cave to partake in the festivities.

"I can't believe they came out!" he exclaimed. For Carter his week of surprises was just beginning.

"OK, the first person who guesses my favorite number between one and twenty-five will be the winner," I'd announce every Thursday afternoon around two o'clock.

"Winner of what?" the students would ask.

"You'll see . . . , " I'd say with a smile.

It usually took just one circle around the room to get the right answer. As luck would have it, Carter won that week.

"Why number seven?" he asked.

"Ever hear of Mickey Mantle?" I replied.

Like Kate, Lady Grey's greatest ally, Carter was usually the last one to be picked up at the end of the day. As a result, we always had time to talk, and he'd eagerly tell me how he wanted to be a writer.

"I'm working on a book right now," he'd say, quite seriously. "It should be finished by the fall."

Toward the end of the week, he began to open up a little more. His stepmother was never around, and his father was in jail, but he was excited because his real mother, who drank too much (but was trying to quit), was going to pick him up today. Of course, she'd never show up, and it was heartbreaking to see the disappointment in his eyes and a slump weigh down upon his young shoulders. Still, he never gave up hope and always defended her.

"She probably had to work late or something," he'd say, both of us knowing that she had most likely forgotten about him because she was drinking again. His heartache made me even gladder that he'd won the contest that week.

The game was simple: Carter would be blindfolded and led by me and the students to a small room a few doors down from the adoptions desk. Before we left the classroom, each student had to give a solemn oath not to give any hints or clues as to where we were going.

Once we arrived at the small room with the orange door, the class had one job to do: not spill the beans. For many it was torture similar to the observation exercise, for what greeted their eyes once they were

Doc

inside was almost too much to bear silently. Through giggles of glee and deep sighs of wonderment, I'd position each student about two feet apart along the perimeter of the room and whisper instructions in their ears as to what I wanted them to do. Remarkably, most of the time, the objects of everyone's affections would remain exceptionally quiet during this setup process, leaving Carter and each week's winners comfortably in the dark regarding their whereabouts and what might happen. I'd then roll out a comfortable exercise mat in the middle of the floor and calmly ask the winning boy or girl to lie down on his or her back.

"The magic is about to begin," I'd announce.

A huge grin spread across Carter's blindfolded face. It had been a rough week for this troubled, heavy-set boy, as he had not been completely accepted by the rest of the group. I was hoping that this experience would help him to remember the week in a brighter and more positive light.

"Carter, are you ready?" I asked. The anticipation for the rest of the class was almost too much to handle. Everyone nodded his or her heads, including Carter.

"Oh, one more thing," I remembered. I removed a fragrant silver packet from my shirt pocket and sprinkled its contents all over Carter's body. He giggled with delight as the tiny particles landed lightly all over his clothes.

"OK, everyone, on the count of three. One . . . two . . . *three!*"

All at once there was a chorus of metallic clinks and aluminum clanks, and before anyone could say a word, a mewing wave of the cutest, hungriest, and friskiest kittens you've ever seen poured out of every cage in the room. Destination: Carter.

Brooks and Dunn, Pepper and Pewter, Freckles and Sunshine, Coca-Cola and Pepsi, they were all there, jumping over his body, tickling his chin, wrestling on his belly, galloping up and down his legs, and crunching kitten chow by his ears. The rest of the class watched in delight as twenty-five kittens covered him like a furry blanket.

"What do you think is going on?" I asked the still-blindfolded Carter, who was now roaring with laughter.

He couldn't answer me. A kitten named Socks was too busy licking his cheeks.

The following Thursday at two o'clock I made an announcement.

"OK, the first person who guesses my favorite number between one and twenty-five will be the winner."

"Winner of what?" everyone asked in unison, except for a smiling, heavy-set boy in the back of the classroom. He'd decided to sign up for another week. I gave him a wink.

"You'll see . . ."

*purr*

# CHAPTER 11

# Midnight

THE DECISION TO MOVE to California was sealed by an outdoor thermometer cupped to an icy kitchen window one mid-January morning.

"What does it say?" Linda asked.

"One degree," I replied.

Linda had lived with me through thirteen East Coast winters in a row, and she was tired of being cold and so far away from her family. She wanted to go home.

"That's it," she snapped. "My turn."

"OK, let's go," I said.

Four months later, after selling most of our furniture and belongings, we rented an orange U-Haul van and headed west. Destination: San Diego.

We had no jobs waiting for us. We had very little money. Through an ad in the Sunday real estate section of a local paper sent to us by a friend, we had found a rundown house in a neighborhood just north of downtown. In exchange for replacing the carpets and giving the interior a fresh coat of paint once we arrived, we'd get two months' free rent.

"I hope there's a pepper tree in the backyard," Linda smiled excitedly as we mailed off the rental agreement. There was no turning back. . . .

"Boy, are we happy to see you!" a short man with peppery hair and aviator glasses beamed as he extended his hand. "Robert Ortega. I live across the street." He pointed to a tidy beige ranch-style house with white shutters. "Welcome to California!"

Linda and Hayden ran up the walkway to greet Linda's mom, uncle, and sister. They'd arrived earlier in the day and had already started cleaning and spackling.

"Hi, Robert. My name is Gary."

I let Squeeze and Brodie out of the cab. They immediately began staking their claim on a row of jade bushes in the front of our new house. A good-size pine tree shaded the sidewalk where I was standing. Its deep aroma was instantly reassuring and familiar.

"I can't tell you how happy we are to see you," Robert started. "We didn't think we'd *ever* get that riffraff out of here," Robert said, tossing his finger toward our house. "Three years of nothing but trouble."

I smiled and told him that we looked forward to becoming part of the neighborhood and started up the front walkway. Linda greeted me halfway. She was grinning from ear to ear.

"There's a pepper tree in the backyard," she said excitedly. "A big, old beautiful pepper tree."

She led me through a small wooden gate by the side yard where amidst the overgrown vines and weeds stood a tall, silver-barked tree with cascading lime-leafed branches and bright red berries.

"Rub the leaves together between your fingers and smell," Linda instructed.

I picked up a willowy bough and gently pulled off a few leaves. The fragrance was pungent and spicy, and the berries, indeed, had a distinct peppery scent.

Inside, the house was a complete disaster. Windows were broken, fists had been put through walls and doors, and the carpeting looked like it hadn't been cleaned in ten years. We'd certainly be earning our two months' free rent over the next few weeks.

In addition to the overall disgraceful condition of the house, our prior tenants had left something else behind as well. We found him sitting on a ledge outside our bedroom window. Linda shot me her patented "last thing we need is another pet" look. Little did we know we'd have scant say in the matter.

Most of the friendly folks who came by to say hello that first day seemed to know the big, black cat that lived at our "new" house. There was little agreement, however, on what his name was.

"Hi, Oreo," said one little girl riding her bike.

"Hi, Blackie," replied a young boy whizzing by on a skateboard.

"Hi, Licorice," greeted a young couple walking their dog.

"His real name is Midnight," piped up a small voice from across the street.

I turned around and noticed a cute little girl of eight or nine sitting on the curb in front of Robert's house. She'd been kind of hanging around all afternoon watching us unload the van.

"I know that for a fact because he used to be my cat before we had to move," she continued.

"Did you used to live here?" I asked.

"Yep," she replied.

"Why didn't you take him with you?"

The girl slowly looked down at her shoes. "Because my mom said he was too much of a hassle." She paused for a moment and looked away.

"What's your name?" I asked.

"Alicia," she replied.

"Well, Alicia," I said, "you can come over and visit Midnight anytime you like."

She lifted her head, and a big smile dawned across her sweet face.

"Thanks!" she said. She ran over to a bicycle that was resting against a telephone pole near Robert's driveway.

"He loves to have his tummy rubbed!" she yelled as she jumped on her seat, searched clumsily for pedals, and rode away.

I have known a few strong cats in my life, but the first time I picked up Midnight, I felt as though I were holding a bowling ball with whiskers. A big, black, imposing tomcat, Midnight carried himself with the swagger of a championship body builder. His short, thick tail and rock-solid backside made him appear even more powerful, and the broad white bib across his hard chest seemed only to be lacking in some kind of super-hero insignia. His large, mustard-colored eyes were as clear and bright as a pair of miniature halogen headlights, and his meringue-dipped front paws and mighty back legs were the perfect finishing touches for that highly tuned hot rod of a cat.

Like his rugged counterpart, Mitten, he did have a few characteristics that undermined some of his macho thunder. For example, his polite meow did not match his girth and stature, and he had the very unflattering habit of drooling uncontrollably when you scratched his back or rubbed his belly. His purr was equally messy—a stuffy, breathy, sinusy snore that resembled an old gasoline lawn mower trying to kick over after a winter in the storage shed. And if you made the mistake of patting him or giving him a scratch or two on the neck, you'd better be prepared to stick around a while. If not, he'd chase you down the sidewalk until you gave him more attention. If you ignored his requests, he'd gladly latch on to your ankle and ride along for a few blocks until you gave in.

If Mitten was the Errol Flynn of our feline family, Midnight was Marlon Brando. And when our swashbuckling transplant from the East Coast arrived in the Godfather's neighborhood that first summer, a turf war erupted that made the South Side of Chicago in the twenties seem like Knott's Berry Farm.

Their fights were legendary, no-holds-barred matches where no one ever gave in or backed down. Their battles would often start in the evening, on the ledge outside our bedroom window, usually just as Linda and I were drifting off to sleep. Midnight was the master of the surprise ambush, the thick-leaved jade plants providing the perfect cover for his burly body. Mitten, on the other hand, had to rely on his quickness and agility to fend off these sudden attacks, and you'd often find him staked out behind a group of terra-cotta flowerpots on the patio or on top of a garbage can.

Many nights I'd stumble into the street in my pajamas and separate the stubborn warriors, exiling Midnight to the garage and sentencing Mitten to the back porch. For all their theatrics, no one ever got seriously hurt or wounded. To them it was grand sport, with the undercarriages of parked cars and rooftops acting as playing fields and showcases for their battle skills and expertise. Mitten usually got the worst of these suburban melees. He'd often show up for breakfast with a fresh batch of nose scratches and ear bites. But he was dogged and relentless in his pursuit for a piece of the action, and he never gave up until the day we left.

We spent five years in that busy suburb of San Diego. But the following fall we were aching for some peace and quiet. As with many East Coast transplants, we had become somewhat disenchanted with the two things that had drawn us to Southern California in the first place—the perfect climate and the laid-back lifestyle. We had grown weary of the cloudless skies and identical days and the endless weeks of sunshine that seemed to pile upon each other like stacks of computer paper. We longed for a midsummer downpour, the orangey autumn glow of an oak-crested hillside, and the powdery touch of snowflakes falling from a pewter sky. The once-easygoing border and Navy town of my wife's youth was now a frantic metropolis, where lives and heartbeats—once set to the rhythms of mariachi bands and the mighty Pacific—were now governed by the nerve-wracking cadences of traffic lights and fast-food drive-up windows.

And so, one weekend in early October, lured by an ad in the local paper and promises of Indian corn, pumpkins, and homemade apple pie, we decided to take a drive to the small mountain town of Julian, situated about fifty miles east of San Diego. We immediately fell in love with the old gold-rush town and found ourselves gazing dreamily at real estate windows, eagerly pointing at sun-curled snapshots of knotty pine living rooms, stone fireplaces, and green pastures. It was a trip that restored our faith in the wild beauty of the West. It also rekindled a desire to take another risk in our restless lives.

Like everyone else in the neighborhood, we immediately fell in love with Midnight. But despite the fact that he became an important member of our family and a treasured part of our daily lives, he seemed to belong to something greater than us. In many ways he would always be the "official" neighborhood cat, loved, recognized, and cared for by everyone. He was also, in this cozy little cul-de-sac, as safe as an outdoor cat could expect to be, something I couldn't begin to promise at our new place in the mountains. So, as difficult as it was, we decided to leave our beloved tomcat behind.

A week before we moved, I walked outside to get the mail. Lying by the front walk, in a self-styled nest of pine needles, was a big black cat soaking up a few rays from the early-morning sun. As I walked in his direction, he acknowledged my presence with a hearty yawn and tucked his head back into his warm chest. I paused for a moment and admired the neighborhood that had been so good to us over the past five years. Midnight got up, meowed, and walked over to brush up against my leg. I sat down on the steps and started scratching his back. As usual, he began to drool. One of Hayden's friends skated by on a pair of roller blades.

"Hello, Midnight," she called.

I picked him up, cradled him in my arms, and rubbed his belly. He purred with delight as another one of Hayden's friends walked by carrying a box full of Barbie dolls.

"Hi, Midnight," she said.

I put him down on the sidewalk, and he strolled across the street. Robert was taking out the trash for the midmorning pickup.

"Hello, Midnight," he said, leaning down to give him a pat. "Sure am glad you're leaving him behind," he called to me. "Don't know what the neighborhood would be like without him."

Midnight

My good friend, Geoff, would be stopping by in a few minutes to pick up the key to the front door. Our landlady was pleased that she'd have another reliable tenant for the coming year.

I started to go through the stack of mail I'd set down on the ledge beneath our bedroom window. Most of it was junk except for a brightly colored envelope. It was a birthday card addressed to Hayden from her grandparents in New York. It would be waiting for her on the dining-room table when she got home from school.

*purr*

CHAPTER 12

## "DADDY, LOOK WHAT WE FOUND!"

The tone of Hayden's voice had that all too familiar ring. The sparkle of hope in her greeting was a sure sign that her treasure was of the living variety. But the look on my wife's face told me something was very wrong, and when she opened up her coat in the dim light of the front porch, I gasped in disbelief.

She couldn't have weighed more than two pounds. I had never seen such a sick cat. I was afraid to touch her for fear I might catch something. Her chin was swollen and bloodied with broken scabs, and her ears were chafed and raw. Her head looked twice the size of her emaciated body, and what once used to be a tail was a hairless whip of flesh and bone. Her sparse coat was pockmarked with barren patches of sores, and when Linda set her down on the sidewalk for a moment to button up her jacket, she toppled over like a toy whose batteries had just given out. Truth was, she was dying.

"Where did you find her?" I asked.

"Across the street, just above the canyon," Linda said. "What are we going to do?"

"Let's bring her inside," I replied quickly.

Taking care not to expose her to any of the other animals for fear of disease, we quickly set up a makeshift shelter out of an old rabbit hutch in the garage. Despite her desperate condition, she showed little interest in food or water. She just stood motionless in the middle of the cage, occasionally listing to one side, like a mortally wounded sea vessel preparing to sink. We doubted that she'd make it through the night.

But when we got up next morning and went out to the garage, she was miraculously still alive, standing in the exact same position we had left her some eight hours before. It was hard to tell if she had eaten or just stepped in her food but that didn't matter to Hayden. She quickly disappeared to go fill a water bowl for the tiny survivor.

"Mommy and I have already picked out her name," she told me authoritatively when she returned.

"Oh, *really?* What did you come up with?" I asked.

"Lucy."

"Lucy? Why Lucy?"

"Because she looks like a Lucy," Hayden said firmly.

"Don't protest too much," Linda added quietly, fully aware of Hayden's current television habits. "Ethel was her first choice."

And so the cat that was almost named Ethel would endure another night and another and then another and eventually become the eighth four-legged member of our family. All of this happened, almost unbelievably, just two days before we were moving up to Julian, California.

The introduction of a new pet into a home can often be an awkward and cranky affair. In those first few days, lines can be drawn that may take months or years to erase. But Lucy's acceptance into our household was different. Perhaps it was due, in part, to the move and the total uncertainty of everything, but for some reason, there was no hissing or barking, no jealous battles or territorial outbursts. It was as if the other animals understood her fragile nature and traumatic past. The swift and gentle approval of her presence in our home was unique and heartwarming.

Over time, it became very clear that there was something wrong with Lucy, that not only was she unusually small and frail, but there seemed to be some deep-seated neurological problems as well. An initial battery of tests and blood work from the vet's office proved inconclusive.

"I'd sure like to climb into her head and see how she views the world," I said to the vet one day as he examined her eyes.

"I'm not sure I'd want to do that," he said dryly. "It could be a very strange place in there."

He was probably right. Her depth perception was completely out of whack. We'd often walk into a room and find her teetering on the lip of a table or countertop, eyes closed, purring contentedly, completely oblivious to the fact that the slightest puff of air or nudge might send her crashing to the floor. Even when she wasn't napping, she'd choose the most precarious spots to observe the daily goings-on of our family.

One evening, as I was preparing dinner, Linda walked into the kitchen.

"Is something burning?" she asked.

"I don't think so," I replied. "I'm just making a salad."

"I smell something burning."

She began combing the house, moving hurriedly from room to room, in search of the source of the smoky odor.

"Now that you mention it, I *do* smell something," I said. "It smells like it's coming from the bedroom."

Linda poked her head in the bathroom and the linen closet as she walked down the hall toward our bedroom. When she reached the doorway, she let out a yelp.

"Lucy! Get away from there!" she shouted.

Perched on the corner of our dresser, directly in front of a tall, green incense candle that Linda had lit earlier, was a little cat with a big depth-perception problem. Linda watched, frozen in amazement, as Lucy sat inches from the flame, completely numb to the fact that her fuselike eyebrows were systematically dissolving across her forehead in tiny puffs of smoke. Linda quickly yanked her away and carried her over to the bed.

"What's the matter?" I called out.

"Lucy's on fire," was her exasperated reply. I dropped a handful of red cabbage on the counter and raced down the hall into the bedroom. There, cradled in Linda's arms, was our nearly eyebrowless cat.

"I think I saved two," she said, pointing to the singed stubs above Lucy's eyes.

"Make that one and a half," I remarked, as another charred tip fell into Linda's lap, like ashes from the end of a cigarette.

Although her depth perception may have been extremely limited when it came to calculating the distance of burning candles and heights of countertops, she was keenly aware of other things, particularly the sound of a front or back door opening. Like Mitten, she was a master of sneaking outside, and the slightest turn of a doorknob or creak of a hinge would send her leaping toward the door. Knowing that she'd have little chance of surviving even one night outside in the mountains, we spent countless hours chasing and retrieving her from the driveway and the meadow. It was a maddening and frustrating routine, and many afternoons and nights upon returning home from work or school, the first words out of everyone's mouth were not "Hi!" or "How are you?" but "Is Lucy inside?"

Remarkably, over time Lucy regained much of her strength and as a result became much more bold and assertive, particularly around the other cats, and her influence on the rhythms of our daily lives became more pronounced. Unlike Rainbow and Mitten, Lucy liked to sleep the entire night. Consequently, by ten o'clock the next morning, she wasn't interested in lounging in cushiony rocking chairs or napping on love seats. She was rarin' to go and looking for some action—and not in the form of playing with a bunch of cute cat toys or balls of yarn. She was hungry for a fracas, a melee, a confrontation.

A showdown.

Fresh from a good night's rest and a belly full of chow, this rejuvenated six-pound, seven-ounce cowgirl would comb the entire house in search of a duel, galloping from room to room, raiding suspected hideouts, ambushing darkened corners of bedroom closets and kitchen pantries for prospective gunslingers to do battle with. With dogs too big and lazy to care, the pool of willing participants was always quite slim. It usually came down to Rainbow or Mitten, with the not-so-brave Rainbow always retreating to the top of an armoire or refrigerator at the slightest hint of a skirmish. That left Mitten, our feline counterpart to Wyatt Earp, to deal with our little Johnny Ringo.

At first he coolly deflected her persistent calls to battle with disinterested yawns and sleepy turns of the head. But as Lucy's provocations became more energetic and pointed, he was forced to acknowledge her challenges and eventually had little choice but to put this diminutive outlaw in her right place.

They finally agreed to meet one February morning. The braided rug in the living room would serve as their O.K. Corral.

Mitten showed up first. He immediately staked a claim on a sunny patch of red and gray braids in the middle of the rug. He sat down and calmly started grooming himself.

Suddenly there was a commotion down the hall and a flurry of gallops. Within moments, a tiny head peered around the doorway. It was Lucinda, *la gatita bandida*. Eyes dilated with anticipation, she crept up the stairs along the oak banister and carefully positioned herself behind the Southwestern-style stuffed chair in the corner, never once diverting attention from her very suspecting rival, who continued to quietly clean himself in the soothing, midmorning light.

Lucy slowly lowered her body to the floor. Then, with neck extended, she wiggled her backside three times and, like a gunshot, exploded toward the deputy. In an exceptional display of timing, awareness, and coordination, Mitten casually stepped to the side, and Lucy flew headlong into the piano bench.

Lucy

Dazed and bewildered, she whirled around and lunged toward him again. With the skill of a master toreador, he sidestepped this second charge, and she disappeared in a tumbling display of paws and claws beneath the ottoman.

She emerged a few moments later, a little dazed and with her whiskers covered in dusty cobwebs. Pulling herself together as best as she could, she prepared for another onslaught. Once again, she lowered herself to the floor, wiggled her backside three times, and leapt towards her prey. This time Mitten held his ground and, in a remarkable demonstration of generosity and restraint, allowed Lucy to barrel straight into his chest. Now face-to-face, he gave her a very calculated bat to the head, admonished her foolishness and persistence with an impressive growl, and left her to ponder her defeat in the middle of the floor.

Lucy would challenge Mitten many times that winter. With each instance I marveled at his patience, kindness, and tolerance. Although he was firm and made it clear when Lucy crossed the line, he was always the forgiving mentor, and there was a tender benevolence to his well-placed swipes and snarls. I loved to watch their fencing matches and will forever remember the sheen of their coats bounding about in the ambitious rays of the morning light.

Eventually Lucy would tire herself out and become the perfect lap cat. On days when I could barely come up with an original idea or single paragraph at the computer, Lucy became my constant writing companion—always showing up to rescue me. Bounding across my keyboard like a circus pony, her dainty paws would send sentences flying and paragraphs scrolling out of control. I'd yell and scream in protest, but deep down I was grateful for the interruption and her ability to make me laugh. Once confident I was back on track, she'd then curl up on my thigh and go to sleep. The idea of disturbing this little ball of tranquillity made it very difficult to escape on those days when I didn't feel like writing. Her steady and loving presence each morning gave me the courage to keep going. Once again, like so many cats in my life, she was my anchor, a gentle tether to a place I needed to be.

One such morning, as I was writing at my desk, with Lucy curled up in my lap as usual, a violent tremor suddenly rifled through her body. She fell to the floor and tried to stand up, but an even more vicious pulse threw her against the wall. Now I have seen a number of dogs have seizures in my life, but I was unprepared and stunned by the force and intensity of these convulsions. And despite an irresistible desire to pick her up and hold her in my arms, I had learned during my tenure at the shelter that to pick up an animal in the midst of this kind of seizure could result in a serious bite or injury. During these episodes, a dog or cat is usually totally unaware of their surroundings. Their responses are strictly physiological, and a set of jaws, no matter how small, could easily clamp down on a hand or arm and not let go. Every instinct screams to reach out and comfort, but one can only watch and wait until the spasms pass.

With each wave randomly flinging her tiny frame against the walls and furniture, I had to find a way to prevent her from hurting herself. I quickly ran into the bathroom and grabbed a large bath towel. I covered her and held her down against the soft carpet, trying to absorb each twitch and shudder with my steady grip in a futile attempt to diffuse their power. After what seemed to be the longest minute and a half of my life, the tremors finally subsided. I gently picked her up, pulled her to my chest, her heart fluttering swiftly in my fingertips. Nestled in my arms and panting from exhaustion, she looked up at the ceiling and, as if awakening from a nightmare, let out a small cry. I held her close, small heart to bigger heart, and wondered how much more this fragile waif could bear.

Once again I took Lucy to the vet. She'd need medication every day to control the seizures, a prognosis that struck fear into my jumpy hands. I had never successfully pilled a cat in my life. Who'd have the patience and be brave enough to venture into the jaws of death, twice a day, for the rest of her life?

"It's cinchy," the vet assured me, as he casually plopped the first pill into Lucy's willing mouth and massaged her throat.

I knew otherwise.

When I returned home from the vet with Lucy's medication, Hayden must've detected the same kind of subtle panic as I had exhibited in the office a little earlier.

"Oh, c'mon, Dad," she said, "it's cinchy."

And for her it was. Twice a day, once before leaving for school and then again before dinner, Hayden would pluck Lucy from a kitchen counter or dresser top and carry her to the middle of the dining-room floor. There she'd sit down and carefully straddle her furry patient, squeezing her thighs and legs together to prevent any possibility of Lucy squirming or running away. She'd then calmly pull the cat's head back, part her lips, and begin boldly poking her fingers around Lucy's heavily toothed gums, fearlessly flirting with sharp fangs and incisors, in an effort to find the perfect place to spot the little white pill. To me, it was like watching someone position a piece of cheese on the spring of a live mousetrap.

But Hayden understood that pill placement was crucial, and the deeper the location, the less likely Lucy would spit it out. Much in the same way a horse can sense assurance in a rider, Lucy's inclination to bite was tamed by Hayden's confidence and resolve. The few times I was in charge of Lucy's medication while Hayden was away on sleepovers were total disasters. You'd think I'd been asked to pill a mountain lion.

It's easy to get lulled into believing that our cats will live forever. We take for granted the nights they sleep by our sides and the moments they curl up in our laps. But I always had a feeling that Lucy's time with us would be short. As a result, I tried extra hard to make her daily life in our home as comfortable and enjoyable as possible. I discovered a peace in my care for her—a serenity in the time I devoted to her. I loved her not only for who she was but for who I became when I was with her. Through Lucy I was able to sample the sweet virtue of unconditional love.

I got the call on a Thursday night in February. I was in the fifth week of a Northeast book tour, and I was staying at my mom and dad's home for a few days. It was Linda.

"We can't find Lucy."

My heart sank. Not only over the fact that she was missing but because I was over three thousand miles away and there wasn't anything I could do. And as much as I wanted to blame Linda and Hayden for allowing Lucy to get out, I knew it wasn't their fault. God knows how many times she'd slipped out the front door between my unsuspecting feet. I asked the usual questions.

"Did you check the garage and the storage shed?"

"Yes."

"Did you look in all the closets and down in the basement?"

"Yes, honey, we looked everywhere," Linda replied. "Here, Hayden wants to talk to you."

"Hi, Daddy."

"Hi, sweetheart."

Her voice sounded small and far away.

"Daddy, we can't *find* her."

I wanted to assure her that she'd come back home and everything would be fine. But I couldn't find those words. So I asked more questions.

"When was the last time you saw her?"

"This morning before I left for school. Maybe some people found her?"

"Maybe, honey."

She started to cry.

"I want you to come home, Daddy."

I stared at a black suitcase that lay open on the floor. Six weeks away from home is a long time.

"Only a few days left to go. Put Mommy back on, sweetheart. I'll talk to you in the morning." Linda got back on the line.

"Well, I've had enough of the 'big, strong mountain woman running the homestead on her own' show. You can come home now," she said impatiently.

"Did you check the laundry room?"

"I told you, we checked everywhere!" she said, her voice rising. "Look, I have to go. Let's talk tomorrow."

I hung up the phone and walked over to the window of my old bedroom and gazed out over the field of glass. A full moon was slowly rising above the silent crest of the great smokestack, and the empty greenhouses below glowed in a milky wash of light. I searched for signs of life in the rows of barren pots on the blacktop, but all was quiet. I knelt down and slowly opened the window. The cold night air felt good on my face.

I took a deep breath and called out the name of a little cat I knew I'd never see again. I closed my eyes and dreamed of a voice soaring west across the snowy Pennsylvania hills into Ohio. A voice sailing above the dormant hayfields and severed corn rows of southern Illinois and Missouri, a voice gaining speed across the frozen copper earth of Oklahoma and New Mexico, rising swiftly above the barren mesas and weathered spires of Arizona. A voice drifting through the backcountry of Southern California, echoing through the hills and funneling up a long drive to a front porch where, beneath the gentle glow of a porch light, a small dish of food would be waiting, all night long.

*purr*

# CHAPTER 13

# Spencer

WHEN I WAS ABOUT SEVEN years old, my mother subscribed to a series of monthly soft-cover nature books that focused on wildlife and fauna from different parts of the United States. Each thin volume came with wax-papered packs of colorful stickers, and it was my job to paste them in the empty boxes next to the corresponding stories.

By far, the region of the country that intrigued me the most was the desert Southwest. With its dangerous and mysterious cadre of scorpions, tarantulas, bobcats, Gila monsters, sidewinders, black widow spiders, and coyotes, it was the most foreboding and foreign of landscapes, and it both scared and thrilled me at the same time. And the fact that Rusty, my perfect dog, had wolf and coyote-like features (my father used to call him "puppy wolf") only made my fascination with that part of the world even stronger. Most of all, I dreamed of hearing the howl of a coyote under a full desert moon.

Some thirty years later, just two weeks after we arrived in California, we headed straight out to the Anza Borrego desert for a weekend camping trip. My goal was simple and clear: to hear the wail of a coyote under that big Southwestern sky.

We arrived at the campsite in the late afternoon. The excited voices of other families unloading coolers and tents from the backs of SUVs and trucks ricocheted off the naked limestone hills ringing the campground, and the warm, dry air funneling down through the stony canyons felt soothing to my ragged, suburbanized nerves. Despite the fact that I was over three thousand miles away from home, the clean, grainy, palomino-tinted sand felt familiar beneath my freshly bared feet, remarkably similar to the sandy soil of Long Island I grew up on, perhaps a little more coarse, but comfortable and knowable nonetheless.

We picked out a spot beneath a willowy acacia tree, and I immediately started a fire for the fresh *carne asada* we'd picked up at the local market. The thin slivers of meat smelled good in the spicy marinade. I could barely wait for the sun to go down.

A little after midnight, after pots and pans had been rinsed and sleeping bags unfurled, I staked out a smooth boulder beyond the glow of campfires and Coleman lanterns, found a foothold, climbed aboard, spread out an old Navajo Indian blanket, eased down cross-legged, and began my vigil. I felt positively ancient in my shamanic outpost, convinced that this would be the night I would finally hear the howl I had dreamed about through those sticky snapshots in my nature booklets. Conditions were prime—a full moon, a light wind, and a crispy, not-too-cold edge to the air.

*Perfect coyote-howling conditions,* I thought to myself. *Tonight's the night.*

Three hours later I hadn't heard as much as a twig snap from the surrounding hills. At about 3:00 a.m., cold and disappointed, I picked up my blanket and limped stiff-legged back to our campsite.

"How did it go out there?" my wife asked drowsily as I crawled into my sleeping bag.

"Damn coyotes," I mumbled.

Not long after, somewhere between trying to fall asleep and wondering what time it was, I heard a rustling sound just outside our campsite. The soft orange glow that was beginning to light up our tent told me that a good night's sleep was a thing of the past, and I struggled halfway out of my sleeping bag to see what was going on. With a charley horse building in my left calf, I reached up to pull down the zipper of the front door flap, trying to be as quiet and stealthy as possible so as not to disturb whatever creature might be visiting our campsite.

"Probably a ground squirrel," I muttered quietly to myself as I pulled the zipper down one click at a time. When I finally peered out through the small, toothy crack, I couldn't believe my eyes. As if special-delivered by some phantom parcel service, there stood six coyotes right outside our tent! Before I could even turn to tap Linda on her leg, one by one, they started to howl, each raising their heads skyward as if posing for a Wild West greeting card or poster, their calls cascading into a ramshackle symphony of yips and yowls as they lightly trotted into the sagebrush. I wanted to leap out of the tent and follow them, but instead I fell back onto my pillow, put my arms behind my head, and basked in the realization of a lifelong dream. Little did I know that it would be the first of many encounters with the species known as *Canis latrans*—the "barking dog."

Three months after we lost Lucy, we moved off the mountain. Dreams of a writer's life on a farm had been dashed by a phone call one February night.

"They've decided to pass on the cat book," my agent said.

"What?" I gasped. "What did they say?"

"Cat books don't sell."

I stayed away from the mountain for a long time. Initially, I was angry over the hard lessons the backcountry had taught me. I understood that cats disappear in the night and dreams fall apart, but what concerned me most was the numbness I felt about a place that had once given me such joy and sanctuary.

The few times I returned to pick up furniture and tie up loose ends, I noticed a disturbing shift in the way I viewed that world up there. Suddenly, all the things that had given me peace and pleasure were not to be trusted. The windswept crowns of the lodgepole pines and cedars, whose gentle whispers had often escorted me to sleep on winter nights, were now nothing more than well-crafted hideouts for sinister birds of prey. The mesquite-covered hillsides, once gorgeous blankets full of simplicity and texture, were now just thorny barracks for packs of coyotes waiting to invade my backyard. The brambly mounds of wild blackberry bushes that dotted the meadow had been transformed into sneaky tents for hungry foxes and weasels, and the brilliant alpine moon was just a ruthless searchlight scouring driveways and decks for easy meals. Truth is that I'd brought Starbucks sentimentality to a wild place and had experienced a swift and raw awakening as to the rules of mountain life.

Three months later I had to return to close a bank account. Although much of my anger had been softened by time and distance, I still felt cautious and closed off to the sweet October air and clear blue sky. I drove by the old farm, still half hoping that I might see Lucy sitting by the front fence or wandering by the road. I turned around in the driveway next door and headed home.

On my way back down the hill, I saw a familiar sign: APPLES AND PEACHES AHEAD. I decided to stop. Meyer's Orchards was a charming fruit-and-vegetable stand about a mile outside of town. In the late summer and early fall, they'd specialize in a fine assortment of apples, peaches, and pears, and their fresh cherry cider was the best I'd ever tasted. I pulled into the parking lot, the crackling gravel announcing my arrival beneath the tires of my old van. A fresh planting of mums in an old wine barrel greeted me as I stepped outside the door.

I picked up a small red basket and walked inside. The plentiful winter rains and mild spring had insured a bumper crop of apples this year, and the green bins that lined the walls were bursting with a bounty of varieties. As I casually bagged a few of each, I noticed a small, white piece of paper tacked on a bulletin board above the Granny Smiths. The scrawled-out message was written in pencil: FREE KITTENS! 6 FEMALES, 10 MALES. ASK FOR MRS. MEYER.

A pleasant, gray-haired woman was handing out samples of cherry cider from behind the counter. I dropped a few more apples into a brown paper bag and walked over.

"Excuse me, are you Mrs. Meyer?" I asked.

"Yes, I am," she replied as she filled another small cup of cider and handed it to a customer.

"Sixteen kittens?"

"Last time I counted," she replied. "Might have lost a couple to the coyotes last night, but if you're interested in taking a look, I live in the green house across the street."

Even though I had had to convince myself that it was a red-tailed hawk that had taken Lucy and that her loss was a natural consequence of what happens when domestic and wild worlds mingle," I was still taken aback by Mrs. Meyer's matter-of-fact attitude regarding her losing the kittens to coyotes, but before I could say anything, she continued.

"Just bang the empty pie pans against the front stoop, and they should come running from all directions. By the way, would you like a sample of our cherry cider?"

"Sure," I said, already knowing that it would taste amazing as always. She handed me the small ribbed cup, and I gulped it down. It tasted cold and good. I paid for my apples and headed across the street.

I walked up the dirt driveway past a few saggy outbuildings and an old, concrete birdbath. I was greeted by a curiously green farmhouse, a sea green color that seemed totally out of place amid the deeper tones of the large canyon oaks and burgundy-barked manzanitas. The front yard was grassless and barren except for the front walkway, which was framed by a scraggly collection of old pie pans, plastic bowls, and dirty dishes. I picked up one of the dented pans and, per Mrs. Meyer's instructions, banged it firmly against the side of the stone patio. Instantly, ten fuzzy heads popped out from beneath the foundation of the farmhouse like hungry little gophers coming out of their holes.

*Looks like one of those damn posters at Hallmark,* I thought, chuckling out loud. A couple of mama cats appeared from behind tree stumps and garbage cans. I stepped toward them, but they quickly retreated. The kittens followed suit by disappearing beneath the farmhouse.

I clanged the pan again, this time against a rusty hand railing. A second set of gray and white snowballs appeared from the backside of the house. This crew was a miniature mewfest, much more curious and bold than the foundation gang.

I sat down on the stonewall and waited for that special connection, that magic bond, that moment of knowing when I could confidently proclaim, "That's the one!" It never happened. So I shrugged my shoulders and went home.

Sometimes we choose our cats. Most times they choose us. This process was going to be a little trickier. I needed some help. So I enlisted Hayden to come back with me the following day.

"You're back," Mrs. Meyer said, looking up at me as she pulled weeds from a lovely flowerbed beneath the cozy MEYER'S ORCHARDS sign. "Brought a little help, I see?"

"Yes," I replied. "Couldn't make up my mind."

"Well, they're still over there. Eating me out of house and home. By the way, the gray and white ones are the males, and the tricolors are the females. Good luck!"

"Thanks," I said, and we started across the street for another look.

We followed the same procedure. Hayden clanged the pan against the railing and a bouquet of cute faces popped up once again. This time, I cued in on a little orange and white female.

"I bet this is what Quiche looked like when she was a kitten," I said to Hayden. "What do you think?"

She didn't answer. I don't think she even heard me. She was being held captive by a collage of kittens gathered at her feet.

"Dad, they're *so* cute!" she gushed. "I want them all!"

I knew how she felt. But I also knew Linda wouldn't be too keen about adding any new animals to our home. "We don't need any more pets!" she had wailed when I told her about our trip up to the mountain. "Three dogs, two cats, and a rabbit are *enough!*" She was probably right. But I needed something to help me with the loss of Lucy. And I wanted it to come from the place where we lost her.

When the kittens realized that we weren't going to feed them, they eased their affections and attentions and returned to the business of chasing grasshoppers and wrestling in the dirt. Hayden and I sat down on the stonewall and watched them as they played, trying to get a feel for their personalities, watching for some special sign that would help us make our choice. We had all but made up our minds about the Quiche-like kitten when from around the corner of the front porch bounded a feisty gray and white prospect with a peach spot under his chin. He boldly walked past us and brushed himself firmly against our dangling legs. He gave a playful swat to the number-one contender resting by our feet and then proceeded to curl up inside an empty water bowl on the front walk for a snooze.

"Dad, that's too cute," Hayden cried. "He's the one, he's the one!"

"Hayden, I really think we should get a female," I hesitated, thinking about how John "Mitten" Wayne might react to a new male gunslinger rolling into his town.

"Maybe he's a she?" Hayden suggested. "Remember what Mrs. Meyer said about the three color cats being female and the males having two colors? He *does* have that little peach spot under his chin. He's probably a girl."

And so, on a cool, mid-October afternoon, a kitten named Spencer made the winding trip down from the mountain to the flatlands by the sea. We named him for the small valley in which he was born and the one-room schoolhouse where I used to teach when we lived in the backcountry—a place where I often taught about the laws of nature and how fickle and unpredictable life can be.

Once he was home, the object of Spencer's affections was, of course, his biggest detractor.

"Just let him into your lap," I'd say to Linda when she'd push him away.

"Just let him out the door," she'd snap back. "I told you I didn't want any more animals. He's only been here a week, and he's completely disrupted the house."

I couldn't argue with her. He'd transformed our well-ordered little animal kingdom into total chaos, and for the next few months it just got worse. Rainbow stopped attending to business in the cat box, preferring to deposit her opinions about our new addition in a corner by the front door. Mitten quickly tired of Spencer's calls to battle and chose to leave town, spending most of his time outdoors in the neighbor's yard hunting gophers. Canyon, our golden retriever, was not at all amused by Spencer's attempts to ride on his back like a circus pony. Even Brodie, a bastion of patience and tolerance, had to give him a snap or two for attempting to chew on her nose during an afternoon nap.

"Don't worry, honey," I assured her. "He'll be much better once we get him fixed."

I can't begin to tell you how many times I've hung my animal problem-solving hat on that simple operation. Canyon was still marking the corners of dressers and couches five years after he'd been relieved of his reproductive capabilities. I have long since stopped believing in spaying and neutering as the ultimate solution for behavioral issues with cats or dogs.

"I know he's a little mischievous," I added. "But don't you think he looks like a pixie?"

"He's a thug," Linda muttered, refusing to budge. She was right. He was a thug. And there was only one thing left to do.

Spencer had to go to jail.

On the day of his sentencing, Spencer showed little remorse. In fact, he didn't even show up for the hearing. He was too busy stealing

Rainbow's food. Little did he know that Judge Linda would be presiding over the bench that day.

The verdict came down quickly. He was sentenced to four months in the back bathroom. Despite Judge Linda's tough reputation, this was a country-club deal. His nicely decorated cell had a private litter box, a sink, a wicker bed, a small window, and a shower curtain for exercise. He'd be fed twice a day and be given porch privileges between the hours of 9 a.m. and 6 p.m. and would be eligible for parole in three months based on good behavior.

Spencer surrendered to authorities without incident the following evening at five o'clock. Upon arriving in his cell, he promptly attacked a roll of toilet paper. It was a long and trying period, but after serving his full sentence, Spencer was granted parole and given full house privileges again.

"I think he's learned his lesson," I said.

"We'll see," Judge Linda replied. "But I doubt it."

Of course, she was right. Soon after his "release," Spencer immediately began to test the boundaries of his newfound freedom. As with Mitten and Lucy, there was no way of keeping him inside. I should have known that bringing a wild kitten down from the mountain and expecting it to quietly lounge on sunny windowsills and sharpen claws on carpeted cat trees was just not realistic. So with the same hope and worry that accompanied handing a set of car keys to a teenage daughter, I stopped fighting the inevitable and accepted the fact that Spencer was going to be spending more time ambushing grasshoppers than sleeping on easy chairs.

What concerned me even more, however, were the coyotes. When it comes to owning small pets in southern California, dealing with coyotes is a way of life. More than once, I'd seen both Mitten and Midnight bolt across the street to the safety of our front porch, fleeing from a bold coyote that had strayed up from the canyon and riverbed below. It's a maddening dilemma—the alternative is living with miserable, restless, housebound cats that are constantly trying to sneak outside. And the fact that their main threat is one of my most favored wild animals only adds to the frustration.

That being said, we always tried to bring Spencer in at night, making a particular effort to get him inside before dusk, when coyotes can become most active. On evenings when he pushed the envelope, I'd comb every inch of the property, frantically calling his name, convinced, as each minute passed, that he'd been scooped up and taken off into the brush. Invariably, just as I was about to give up, I'd turn around to see him calmly sitting off by himself and watching me, slightly out of sight on a patio chair or under a garden bench, knowing full well that he'd been blithely observing my frenzied search the whole time.

"Thanks a lot," I'd scold him breathlessly while lifting him up into my arms. "Do you get some sort of sadistic pleasure watching me run around like an idiot?" He'd look at me, unfazed, and then I'd remember how casually he had tortured a bewildered field mouse for the better part of an hour on the front porch that morning.

"Never mind," I'd mutter while carrying him back into the house.

On days when I knew we wouldn't be back by dark, I'd attempt to keep him indoors for the entire day, usually with little success. Such was the case one Thanksgiving morning while I was packing up the car with potato salads and apple pies for a holiday visit with Linda's family. When I backed out of the front door, arms filled with hot, aluminum-foiled platters and plates, Spencer managed to slip out beneath my shuffling feet. Despite attempts to get him back into the house before we left, he was nowhere to be found.

Pulling out of the driveway that morning, I had a slight sickly feeling in my gut, angry and disappointed that I hadn't been able to corral our stubborn little felon. I hoped that he'd stay close to the house, and I tried to ease my nervousness by telling myself that he'd be fine and I'd find him when we returned.

When we arrived home that night, I began my customary patrol. I searched the usual spots—peering over neighbors' fences and scouting the church parking lot behind our house. I even broke out the flashlight, hoping to catch the wild flash of his eyes mirroring back at me in the bushes and tall grass that lined our drive. *"Spencer . . . Spencer!"* I called and called, but he never came. After about a half-hour search, tired and frustrated, I went to bed, hoping that I'd be greeted by his hungry face at the front door the next morning.

He never came back.

I knew about the threadlike dirt trail that snaked behind our garage, one of Spencer's favorite places to hunt for gophers. In the kind of irrational dialogue that only comes with being a long-time pet owner, I had warned him time and time again about the dangers of going back there. Of course, he never listened, and in recent months construction across the street from our house had pushed the coyotes even closer to the open fields surrounding our yard. Occasionally, I'd see them skulking beneath the streetlights in the church parking lot, occasionally calling to each other and setting off a barrage of barks and howls from what seemed to be every dog in the neighborhood. With our dogs always at the ready and with all the activity in our yard and driveway, I always thought they'd keep their distance. I was wrong.

Three days passed, and there was still no sign of Spencer. Even though I had resigned myself to the fact that he had most likely been taken by a coyote, I still wanted proof. So I began to walk the fields adjacent to my house, looking for some kind of sign or clue as to what happened. Frankly, I didn't even know what I was looking for, but it felt good to be doing something, if only to walk off some of the anger that was building inside me.

After about twenty minutes, under the hot midday sun, I found an area of flattened and worn-down grass just beyond the church playground. There, in the middle of the matted circle, was a small tuft of

Spencer

gray and white fur. A few feet away I found another wisp of white, gently waving in the wind. I knelt down for a moment, bowed my head, and swallowed hard. Life sure can be messy sometimes.

I walked back home, calmly gathered half of my coyote figurines from the hutch, dumped them into a plastic bag, and headed out behind the garage. I set the bag on the ground, reached in, and, one by one, smashed each of them up against the wall. Those that bounced of the concrete intact were privy to an even more intense and pointed firing. About midway through my thinning out of the pack, I heard a car pull up. It was my friend Greg.

"I don't mean to pry," he quipped sarcastically, "but what the hell are you doing?"

"Damn coyotes killed Spencer," I yelled, while in the middle of a major-league windup. A particularly large and cartoonish wooden figurine was about to meet its maker.

"It's nothing personal, you know," he replied, not really knowing how to respond appropriately. "That's just what coyotes do."

"I know," I said, flinging it against the wall, where it splintered into a dozen pieces. "It just feels good to break a few things."

I reached in the bag and pulled out an old, weathered ceramic coyote with one broken ear and a chink off its turquoise shoulder. Underneath, it said: "To Daddy, Love, Hayden." I paused for a moment.

"You like tuna salad?" I asked my friend while picking up the plastic bag.

"Sure," he said.

"Let's go eat," I replied. "I'm starving."

*purr*

# Clementine

CONSIDERING THE NUMBER OF wayward creatures that have found their way to our front door throughout the years, I've determined that Linda and I must have invisible stamps on our foreheads that only animals can see. The stamps read: *Yes, we're suckers, and we'll take you in and love you no matter what.*

How else could you explain monthly solicitations to our little hidden bungalow on the hill? How come they never go next door to our much more convenient and accessible neighbor's house? And to make matters even more puzzling, these routine drop-ins are not only limited to canines and felines. One day while Linda was gardening in the backyard, a bright green parakeet landed on my wife's head. To this day he lives a life of chirping contentment and luxury on top of our Sears refrigerator.

Another vagabond strolled into our yard late one Friday afternoon from the same place we lost Spencer—the grassy lot behind our garage. A new stockade fence, installed by our neighbors to the west, had seriously impacted the migration cycle of coyotes through our property, so I wasn't quite as worried or concerned about her safety when she first rebuked our efforts to find out whom she might belong to. She was strikingly beautiful—an arresting blend of whites, caramels, and charcoal grays—and her tiny mew was both sweet and heartbreaking. Since she had no collar or identification tag, Linda and Hayden decided to call her Clementine.

"Because she looks like a Southern belle," was their explanation.

Like most strays, she was extremely thin and wary and stayed tucked in a corner beneath the safety of my small boat trailer in the driveway for almost two weeks. I finally got her to come out by offering a handful of kitty chow in a small ceramic dish that I temptingly jangled as she moved ever closer each day. Oddly enough, when she finally felt safe enough to come to me, she seemed more interested in neck scratches and back rubs than food. From the emaciated looks of her, you would have thought she would have devoured every morsel. But she seemed quite content to sample a few bites and then turn to me for as much affection as she could get.

Despite her endearing cuteness and indoor demeanor, Linda immediately dubbed her as "our outside barn cat."

"But we don't have a barn," I remarked.

"Then she'll be our outside garage cat," she quickly replied, emphasizing the "outside" part, knowing fully well that it was just a matter of time before both Hayden and I would start lobbying for our new friend to become an inside fixture instead.

As a compromise, I set up a temporary foster home, complete with a comfy pillow bed and feeding station, in our basement next to the laundry room. With the gas furnace in the corner, it would be plenty warm for Clementine during the chilly winter months, and the thick concrete walls insured a cool shelter from the hot summer days of July and August.

The space also provided protection against the gang of feral cats that had infected Mitten. And despite the fact that I provided her with plenty of food and water, her new digs gave her unlimited access to her favorite source of nutrition—fresh lizard meat.

Yes, whereas Mitten hunted lizards strictly for sport, Clementine's pursuit of the small, blue-bellied reptiles was for reasons of nourishment and table fare. She had remarkable hunting and foraging skills, leaping off the front-porch chair at the slightest bristle of a dry leaf in the tall grass or movement on a windowsill. More than once, I'd walk outside to find her casually gnawing on a lizard tail like a fresh piece of beef jerky.

It bothered me to see these harmless and colorful characters fall prey to Clementine's appetite, but their availability was probably the only reason she had survived for as long as she did. It was another example of how morally and practically conflicting the life of an outdoor cat can be. And with our impending move to the high desert, there was no way she could enjoy the same freedom and outdoor privileges she had in the relatively safe confines of our cozy, suburban neighborhood. Knowing the battles I had with Mitten and Lucy in trying to keep them indoors when we moved to the mountains, how could I possibly turn a lizard-eating, moonlight-bathing stray into a happy house cat?

The chances of a cat that wanders into your front yard being spayed or neutered and up to date on all its shots is highly unlikely. So a few days before we moved back up to the highlands, we decided to take Clementine to the vet for a checkup. There was no way she was going to be an outdoor cat in the high desert. Nothing like offering up the visual equivalent of a cookies-and-cream hot-fudge sundae to the resident coyotes.

"She looks more like a cookie-dough-and-vanilla ice cream cone with a splash of chocolate fudge and caramel," my daughter decided.

Whatever ice cream special she resembled, she needed to be spayed, at the very least, to improve the odds of her converting to indoor life.

Now with a male cat it's quite easy to tell if it's been neutered.

"Can't see 'the boys,' my father used to say when a male cat wandered into our yard sans his feral jewels.

With a female, particularly a long-haired cat, it's a more difficult diagnosis for the layman. So I took Clementine to the local spay/neuter

Clementine

clinic to find out if she'd be bearing a batch of kittens anytime in the future. On my way there, I remembered a dinner conversation my mom had started when I was ten years old about cats "coming into season."

"I think Sweet Kitty is in heat," my mother announced while serving up some homemade pot roast.

"She's got the heat?" my younger brother asked.

"Yep," my father chuckled. "she's got the heat."

I remember excusing myself from the table, running half panicked into the living room to check on Sweet Kitty, who was curled up, sleeping, on the cobbler's bench. I picked her up and immediately felt her forehead. She didn't feel particularly warm. She seemed fine to me. Whatever this "heat" was, it didn't seem to be too serious. So I ran back into the kitchen and queried my mom, who was washing the dishes.

"Mom, what's the heat?"

To this day, I can't remember if she answered me. I do remember that she dropped a glass in the sink, and it broke. But it doesn't matter.

What does matter is that two months later, Sweet Kitty had three kittens under my parents' bed.

"The only way girl cats can have kittens is if they get the heat," Eddie Wilcox, the neighborhood eighth grade authority on everything, told me one day at the bus stop.

"I know that," I said confidently, as the big, yellow school bus pulled up. "I definitely know that."

So when the vet greeted me in the examining room shortly after I walked into the office, I was tempted to ask him if my cat had "the heat"—but I resisted.

"If there're no obvious behavioral symptoms or if we can't find a visible scar or an incision," the vet explained while calmly examining Clementine's teeth, "then the only way we can tell is by going in."

"What kind of behavioral symptoms are we talking about?" I asked.

He handed me a sheet of paper. The heading read *Five Telltale Signs that Your Cat Is in Heat.*

"Take a look at that, and I'll be right back," he said, walking out of the examination room.

I quickly scanned the information before returning to the top of the page. Telltale Sign #2 featured a little too much information for someone who had just finished a ham-and-Swiss-cheese sandwich for lunch.

> 2. *The Queen may also spray vertical surfaces with a strongly scented fluid. She will accomplish this by backing up to the surface and raising her tail high. The tail may quiver, and she may perform the rhythmic treading. . . .*

Thankfully, the vet came back into the exam room before I could read the third sign.

"Do all cats that haven't been spayed exhibit these behaviors?" I asked, casually waving the list in the air.

"Not necessarily," he remarked while feeling around Clementine's furry belly. "Sometimes the behavioral changes can be very subtle. And I'm not seeing or feeling any scars or incision marks here. I think the only way we're going to find out is by going in." I gave him the thumbs up for the "exploratory spaying procedure." He told me to come back around three o'clock and whisked Clementine away.

Three o'clock came, and I was back in the office, right on time.

"Hi, can I help you?" a pretty young girl asked from behind a counter dotted with dishes of hard candy and brochures about West Nile virus.

"Yes, I'm here to pick up my cat, Clementine."

She thumbed through a thick stack of folders on her desk. "Oh, here it is," she said, pulling it out from the pile. She glanced over the chart and then looked up at me. "Hmmm. . . . There's a note saying the doctor wants to see you. I'll be back in a minute."

She disappeared into the back of the clinic as my overactive brain began to analyze what "the doctor wants to see you" meant. Finally she returned and said he was ready to see me.

"Come on in," he said, motioning to the accordion-like door which he slowly slid closed behind him.

"How did everything go?" I asked in my steadiest voice.

"Well," he smiled. "Somebody had already taken care of her spaying. As I told you before, since there were no visual incision marks, there was no way I could tell unless I went in. But she's definitely been spayed, apparently when she was quite young."

A wave of relief washed over me. I silently scolded myself for, once again, projecting the worst.

"Well, how do you like that?" I chuckled, quickly pulling myself together. "By the way, how old do you think she is?"

"I'd say barely a year," he replied.

"Really?" I said.

"Yep," he continued. "And honestly, I was quite surprised to find so much fat in and around her belly. Have you been feeding her a lot?"

I thought of her open buffet in the basement and how easily she went through almost a bowl of chow a day.

"Well, she does have a healthy appetite," I responded.

"You might want to cut back a little," he said. "She's quite overweight. In any case, while I was in there, I took care of those excess pockets of fat deposits."

I looked at him for a moment, somewhat puzzled. And then I realized what he was telling me. Clementine, as they say in Beverly Hills, had "had some work done."

"Are you telling me that you gave my cat liposuction?" I asked.

"Essentially yes," he replied. "She'll be a little sore for a couple of days until the swelling goes down. But after that I think you'll notice that she won't have that sagging belly anymore."

I've heard of people buying fancy collars, leashes, even sweaters for their pets. I have friends who routinely take their cats and dogs to fancy day spas and grooming salons. But this is the first time I'd ever heard of cat cosmetic surgery. I certainly couldn't let my pals back in New York hear about this.

"Yo, Gary, instead of having her de-clawed, have you thought about French tips?"

---

I WALKED OUT FRONT TO the receptionist to pay the bill and wait for Clementine. The young girl behind the counter handed me a printout from her computer as another young girl carefully brought me the beige cat carrier that contained Clementine. I peered through the small cage door at my pretty groggy-looking cat, and we headed for home.

"Oh, one more thing." I said, just before I walked out the door. "Next month, when I bring Clementine in for her teeth cleaning, I think we'll pass on the tummy tuck and boob job."

IF I WERE TO LIST THE career paths of my cats based on their personalities, their choices would be quite diverse. Mitten, with his dedication to defending honor and territory, would surely have gone into law enforcement. I can't imagine Midnight not ending up center stage at Madison Square Garden doing battle as a professional wrestler, his burly frame routinely leaping off of turnbuckles and ropes on the fringes of the squared circle (he would, of course, been known as Captain Midnight). Lucy would have had at least a supporting role in "One Flew Over the Cuckoo's Nest" and Spencer's rebellious demise would have been the perfect subject for any punk rock documentary from the 80's. Rainbow, and her fondness for the Morning Glory family of hallucinogens would undoubtedly have gone the way of many an eccentric beat poet or abstract artist, most likely never leaving her San Francisco flat except to stock up on cigarettes, diet Pepsi, and Hot Pockets.

Most obvious would be Clementine, who in true entrepreneur spirit, has designed her own signature vocation, that of "Professional Luxuriator." With her southern belle grace and manners, she has redefined relaxation in our home with her unflappable commitment to comfort and leisure. While some cats with the same pursuit might be deemed as fat and lazy, her pursuit of the comfortable life is more economical than extravagant and she is deeply committed to finding the perfect lounging spot. In summer, you'll often find her straddling both the kitchen and living room floors, her body strategically spread-eagled on a cool linoleum square or two and her head nestled knowingly on the soft green edge of carpet separating the two rooms. A pair of my daughter's leather pumps may also serve as a fashionable yet practical headrest for a late afternoon nap and awhile back, while curled up on my desk during a writing session, I watched as she sleepily reached out with one of her paws to pull my well-worn wallet underneath her soft, white chin to use as a pillow.

"Well, you were obviously a human in your past life," I said as she positioned her head accordingly. "Would you mind telling me who that might have been?"

She looked up at me for a moment and blinked contentedly, obviously quite pleased with her new, personal head cushion.

"Next time I'll put some singles in there to fluff it up a bit," I promised, not quite believing what I had seen. She had obviously taken quite well to living the house cat life. There was, however, one glaring exception—the taming of her wild palate.

ONE MORNING, WHILE Clementine was rejecting, yet again, another plate of thoughtfully purchased canned cat food, I started off on a tirade about her ridiculously picky eating habits. Linda immediately cut me off.

"You should talk, Morris," she laughed.

"What?" I objected. "I'm not picky. I just have discriminating tastes."

"Oh, really?" she chuckled. "I wouldn't categorize picking out pieces of celery from a deli-made tuna-salad sandwich as 'discriminating.'"

She was right. I am a picky eater. One would think, though, that a homeless cat would be filled with gratitude for just about any offering of food. Not Clementine. The dry food is not the issue. It's the canned food that's the problem.

"I don't understand why you even bother with the canned stuff," Linda says. "The dry food is fine."

It probably is. But despite the fact that their chow bowl is always kept fresh and full, when it comes time to feed the dogs, the cats always gather around anticipating a little something extra for them as well.

The something extra for the dogs is a couple spoonfuls of their favorite canned food to go along with the dry stuff. For me, the idea of randomly throwing some dry food in a bowl with a little tap water is kind of mindless and carefree. I like preparing something special for them. God knows, they're worth it. And if you saw the look on our little terriers face when we've saved the morning bacon drippings for her dinner, you'd probably do the same.

I WISH I COULD SAY that appeasing Clementine's palate is equally simple and satisfying. It's not. Finding the right kind of canned cat food for her is like playing the dollar slots in Vegas. Most of the time you're going to lose.

A few weeks back I found some expensive organic canned cat food on sale at a discount store. The sign read: FOR A LIMITED TIME! 3 CANS FOR $1. Jackpot! You would have thought that all my problems in life had been solved. There, in an overflowing bin, was every flavor combination imaginable and then some—organic roasted chicken in natural gravy, organic beef slices with vegetables, and organic breast of turkey with cheddar cheese strips. I half expected to see a can of braised duckling in caramel and cherry marinade.

I loaded my cart with about fifty cans, fully convinced that there was no way that Clementine could resist such a bounty of selections and flavors. I couldn't wait to get home to prepare her first organic meal.

They say that all those fancy, colorful fishing baits and lures you see at Bass Pro Shops and Cabela's don't catch fish, they catch people, and that some of the most effective baits are really quite plain and unassuming in appearance and presentation. I'm afraid to say that I fell into the same trap with the organic cat food. I was positive that since it sounded good to me, it was going to taste equally as good to Clementine. (I did pass on the chicken and tuna pasta casserole—I draw the line at serving my cats fettuccine.)

Come dinnertime that evening, I opened the pantry door and casually perused the wide selection of neatly stacked feline fare with the same deliberation that comes with choosing a fine Bordeaux at a fancy French restaurant. I decided to go with the organic chopped sirloin slices in gravy.

Clementine was already parked on the kitchen counter as I hooked my finger inside the metallic ring on the aluminum cat-food cover and slowly peeled it away to reveal an irresistible serving of "prime and tender" cuts of beef. I carefully spooned out a small portion into her favorite dish and confidently placed it at her feet, fully expecting her to dive in immediately and not come up for air until she had licked her plate clean. She leaned over, sniffed the dish twice, and then looked up at me.

"You better eat that!" I warned. "That's organic beef!"

She stared at me for a moment, sniffed the dish one more time, turned around, and lazily plunked herself down next to the fruit bowl at the end of the counter.

"Fine," I grumbled, while scraping her meal into the garbage. "Have a banana."

You might wonder why I so hastily threw out her dinner. Two reasons: First, you get one shot with Clementine. Once she rejects a meal, there is no reconsideration at a later date. Kind of like the one-hundred-meter dash at the Olympics. You get one shot, and that's it. That's why, at first, I always give her a sample dollop instead of a big portion. The second reason is because of something that has plagued cat owners for decades, particularly in warmer climates. I'm talking about ants—cat food and ants.

I can't begin to scrape the surface of how many times I've walked sleepily into a kitchen, garage, or laundry room to find a four-lane highway of ants feasting on a bowl of chow or canned cat food. Where I live, in the high desert, they are particularly efficient and voracious, usually sending out scouts at the slightest fragrance or presence of a leftover tidbit or morsel. In the summer, you can't leave anything out on the counters, even for a minute.

Despite assurances of the nontoxic nature of many alternative pest solutions, I've always been extra cautious as to what I use around the house because of the dogs and cats. That being said, when it comes to natural pest control and protecting cat food, I've tried just about everything, including tea-tree-oil solutions, clove and garlic brews, talcum and borax-powder mixes, crushed spearmint leaves, cayenne pepper, and all the citrus oils. Each provides short-term relief at best.

Fortunately, I was able to salvage the remaining forty-nine cans of organic cat food by reassigning their nutritious contents to the normally fussy Rainbow, who seems particularly fond of the more stewy types of turkey and chicken dishes. As for Clementine, even though she still shows up every morning and evening for some kind of special treat, her main diet now consists of a high-end dry food and the occasional dollop of freshly opened canned food, out of which she will lap up only the gravy or sauce, leaving me to tend to the dried-up slivers and squares of naked meat before the ant brigade shows up.

This all may seem tedious and compulsive in its attention and time investment. But it's a very fair trade, an entertaining distraction from the worldly things I have so little control over. And despite the occasional frustrations surrounding finicky appetites, I have found little that matches the satisfaction I get from providing comfort for my loving and devoted fleet of cats, dogs, and horses.

Now if only Purina would come out with a lizard-and-mixed-grill entrée. . . .

*purr*

# CHAPTER 15

# Sir

THERE IS HARDLY A MORE delightful time in a father's life than
when a daughter is between the ages of five and eleven years old. In her
eager and innocent eyes, a dad can do little wrong, and the mutual ease
and adoration that is shared during those years is one of the true trea-
sures of fatherhood. But it is a fleeting bounty, and I still remember the
day when everything changed.

We had recently moved up to the mountain, and Hayden had just
started sixth grade. Our new country home was about a quarter-mile
away from the bus stop, and for the first few days we walked together,
admiring our new neighborhood and the gold and crimson colored
leaves of fall that framed the winding road. But one morning, just before
we came into view of the bus stop, Hayden hesitated and slowed down.

"This is far enough, Dad," she said. "I can walk the rest of the way
by myself."

There is no preparation for moments like that. No matter how
many books you read or stories you hear about daughters growing up,
it always comes as a shock when they take their first hard steps toward
independence.

Feigning steadiness in my voice and heart, I said OK, and we hugged
each other in a way that was brand new—a short and obligatory embrace

that was tempered by the road up ahead and whether we were in the sight of her new friends.

"Bye, Dad," Hayden said as she turned and headed up the hill.

"See you later, honey," I replied.

Weak-kneed and with eyes filling up with tears, I started back down toward the house. Just as I was about to walk up the driveway, I turned and looked back up the hill one more time. There was Hayden, her backpack strapped snugly onto her small shoulders, walking steadily toward the bus stop on her own. Suddenly, she stopped and turned around and looked at me one more time.

*I'm sorry, Daddy,* it seemed she tried to tell me with her pretty blue eyes. And then she disappeared around the bend.

The next six years were as tumultuous as the previous half-dozen had been golden. A newfound awkwardness replaced the easy comfort between us, and the most routine of conversations or exchanges were now breeding ground for arguments and shouting matches. The more distant she grew, the more rigid I became. And even though friends older and wiser than me promised that she'd come back around, it was hard to imagine that she'd ever seek counsel and guidance from me again. Fortunately, there was one bridge that seemed immune to all the breaking away and letting go, something we could always talk about—our cats and dogs.

So you can imagine my delight when Hayden called a short time after her twenty-first birthday from her new apartment and told me that she'd adopted a nine-year-old tabby: her first cat. By far and away, the cats that are most overlooked at the shelter by people and families looking to adopt are the older cats. While kittens and juveniles are often whisked away within weeks of their arrival, many older cats might have to wait a year or longer to find a home. I was ecstatic that she had chosen an older feline companion.

"What's his name?" I asked, when she called to tell me the news.

"Tigger," she said. "But we've already changed his name to Sir."

Sir

Having a very clear understanding about Hayden's reasons and resolve when it comes to naming cats (Rainbow, Mitten, and Lucy come to mind), I queried the inspiration for her latest choice cautiously.

"Sir, eh?" I said.

"Actually," she said, "Winston [her boyfriend] came up with the name. When we first got him, every time Winston walked into a room and saw him, he said, 'Hello, sir.' So that's what we decided to name him."

Ah, the beautiful part in naming cats—anything goes.

Truth is, considering that cats can easily live into their late teens, at nine years old, Sir is barely middle-aged. And for those who think that older cats are dull, lethargic, and that they won't bond with their new owners, think again.

"He was really shy in the beginning," Hayden said after their first week with their new addition. "But now he has kind of taken over the whole apartment."

It wouldn't be the first time a newly adopted cat would trick inno-cent owners into believing that those first days of shyness and timidity was their true personality. More often than not, once new cats get their bearings and confidence back, it's a whole new ballgame. And while it may be advertised that cats are easier and more convenient to take care of than dogs, the moment you bring even the mellowest cat into your home, life becomes more complicated. Good cat food isn't cheap, veterinary bills can be unexpected, and whether it be in a bowl of cereal or all over a brand new sweater, there's *no* part of your life that cat hair won't find its way into. Then there are the cat boxes. Despite the latest formulas and technologies, they'll forever remain one of the most disgusting necessities ever invented by man.

But I wouldn't have it any other way. And neither would Hayden.

Now, despite images of low-maintenance cats sleeping peacefully on sunny windowsills or tucked inside blankets on easy chairs in front of warm fires, some do seem to crave more attention than others. And while there's a general perception that cats are independent and self-sufficient, some can be downright needy.

Enter Sir.

"Don't get me wrong, Dad," Hayden said. "We really love him. But it's almost like having a baby."

I laughed out loud. Hayden pressed onward.

"I'm serious, Dad," she said through my chuckles. "He wants attention all the time. And if you don't give him attention, he'll just sit and stare at you until you do. And it's not like he's just looking at you. He doesn't move, he doesn't blink, and he just keeps on staring at you until you pet him. Winston and I call it 'Creepy Eye Contact Syndrome.'"

Lucy used to stare at me the same way. It *is* creepy.

"He's also a compulsive meower," she continued. "He meows all of the time—in the morning on the end of the bed when he wants breakfast, on my desk when I'm working on the computer. I can't even go to the bathroom without him meowing outside the door. He even meowed in the middle of a yawn the other day. And you know how most cats will rub up against you when they're hungry or want attention? Well, Sir head-butts you instead. Like a mountain goat."

I sure know about cats that want breakfast.

"Does he sleep with you?" I asked.

"I wish!" she said without hesitation. "We have this really ugly chair that we want to get rid of, but it's the only thing Sir will sleep on. And there has to be a piece of my clothing on the chair that he can use for his bed or he'll meow all night long."

I kept asking questions. This, after all, was my very first grand-kitty. "Does he like to be held?"

"Only if you hold him on your shoulder, like you're trying to burp a baby," she said.

Maybe the new baby comparison wasn't so far off.

On the more placid side, in Sir, Hayden has found a dedicated sprawler who has no qualms about spreading out across the entire upper half of her body while she's reading or watching television. Occasionally, he'll just collapse atop the front of her shoulders and neck, taking on the appearance of an oversized scarf or mink stole.

"He'll just camp out and purr on Winston's chest for an hour while he's studying," she says. "It's like all he cares about is being close to us."

There's an old wives' tale that says that cats can jump on your chest in the middle of the night and "steal your breath" while you're sleeping. To me, it's just another in a series of myths and lore designed to help perpetuate the idea that cats are "dark, mysterious, and mystical" animals. As far as I'm concerned, if you're lucky enough to find a cat that's willing to curl up on you lap or chest and purr your troubles away, you've hit the jackpot. There have been many times in my life where the purr of a cat has made things right. My once-in-a-lifetime cat, Mitten, rescued and restored my body and mind regularly throughout his good life, generously jumping up and settling down in the middle of my chest at the slightest indication of a sigh or difficult day—his steady purr recalibrating frayed nerves and runaway hearts. I truly believe that it's only a matter of time before we learn that one of our deepest and greatest healing resources is curled up on the end of our beds.

When Hayden told me that Sir had been declawed, a ripple of anger raced up my spine. If your Ethan Allen sofa is more important to you than your cat, then don't get a cat. Declawing can be an extraordinarily painful and behaviorally scarring ordeal—a completely unnecessary procedure rooted in the expectation that pets are supposed to fit unobtrusively into our lifestyles. Chances are good that the memories and gifts you'll receive from a beloved family cat will far outweigh those of your La-Z-Boy recliner.

Last week, I was able to help walk Hayden through her first kitty crisis, a dilemma that I was all too familiar with.

"I went out and bought all this cat food for Sir, and he won't eat any of it," she wailed.

Visions of Clementine danced through my head. Like many cats before her, a finicky eater was holding my daughter hostage. I talked her off the ledge.

"OK, honey, where are you?" I said calmly.

"I'm at the supermarket," she said.

"OK, that's good," I replied. "Now I want you to walk over to the cat food aisle."

"I'm already there," she said.

"Will Sir eat any chow?" I asked.

"He won't touch it," she replied.

To think that I have a well-defined war chest of cat food feeding strategies might seem odd and possibly disturbing to anyone who doesn't have cats. But to those of us who have seen our cats continually reject plates and bowls of food, it can be a very stressful daily impasse—and a costly one at that—especially for daughters trying to make it on their own.

"OK," I continued. "Find the Friskies canned food section."

"I see it," she said.

Using Clementine's ultra picky palate as a measuring stick, I ran down my list of suggestions.

"First, we'll have to determine if Sir prefers the solid kinds of cat food—the supreme suppers, the mixed grill, the poultry platters, and the like, or the more gravy- based sliced or carved dishes: the prime fillets of beef, turkey, or chicken . . ."

"What about salmon and ocean whitefish?" Hayden asked.

"You can try a can of seafood or two," I replied, knowing that Clementine wouldn't touch any fish dish, even if she were starving to death. "Sir might love them."

"Thanks, Dad," she said, sounding relieved. "I love you."

"I love you too, honey," I answered softly, smiling on my end of the phone.

It's good to be a dad.

*purr*

# Epilogue

ONE NIGHT, WHEN HAYDEN was about six years old, she wheeled her red and orange plastic shopping cart into the living room. Sitting in the cart, on a pink crocheted blanket that her grandmother had knitted for her, was her favorite cat in the whole world. She strolled around the room for a few minutes, pretending to pluck items off imaginary shelves stacked against the walls. Occasionally, she'd stop and ask Mitten for his advice on a particular brand or purchase. When she was finished, she rolled her cart over to me and started to "unload" her groceries.

"That will be $28.32, young lady," I said, smiling and holding out my hand.

She reached into her purse and carefully gave me her invisible currency.

"Out of thirty dollars, that's one and sixty-eight cents makes thirty. Thanks for shopping at Daddy-Mart."

"Thank you."

"By the way, is that your kitty?"

"Yes," she replied shyly. "That's Mitten."

"Well," I said, "I think that's the prettiest kitty I've ever seen."

Hayden blushed and smiled the biggest smile any father could wish for. She waved goodbye and started to head back to her room. All of a sudden she stopped, turned around slowly, and, unable to hold back tears, began to cry.

"What is it, honey?" I asked, confused.

Hayden and Mitten

She walked back over to me and climbed into my lap. I held her for a few moments in silence as she struggled to come up with the right words. Finally, she wiped away the tears dripping down her cheeks and continued.

"Daddy, sometimes when I hear about a kitty dying, it makes me feel worse than when I hear about a person dying. Is that wrong?"

She started to cry all over again, and I pulled her close. A few feet away I saw the best friend any little girl could have, curled up on a blanket inside a small plastic shopping cart.

"No, honey," I said, "there's nothing wrong with that at all."

*purr*

# About the Author

Gary Shiebler is an award-winning singer and songwriter who has produced and written for such country-music legends as Tanya Tucker, Bobby Bare, George Jones, Patty Loveless, Merle Haggard, and Porter Wagoner to name a few. His love for animals—especially dogs, cats, and horses—and his work as a humane educator at the nationally recognized Helen Woodward Animal Center in southern California inspired him to write *The Power of Purrs* and *The Power of Paws*. He lives with his wife Linda and daughter Hayden in Anza, California, with a host of critters that includes two horses, two dogs, two cats, and one cranky cockatiel.

*purr*